JOHN ILHAN
a crazy life

Stephen Dabkowski
& Annie Reid

With Karen McCreadie

WILEY

John Wiley & Sons Australia, Ltd

First published 2010 by
John Wiley & Sons Australia, Ltd
42 McDougall Street, Milton Qld 4064

Office also in Melbourne

Typeset in Bembo 12.2/15.7pt

© Stephen Dabkowski and Annie Reid 2010

The moral rights of the authors and contributor have been asserted

National Library of Australia Cataloguing-in-Publication entry:

Author:	Dabkowski, Stephen.
Title:	John Ilhan: a crazy life / Stephen Dabkowski, Annie Reid.
ISBN:	9781740311021 (pbk.)
Notes:	Includes index.
Subjects:	Ilhan, John.
	Crazy John's.
	Businessmen—Australia—Biography.
	Immigrants—Australia—Biography.
	Retail trade—Australia.
Other Authors/Contributors:	
	Reid, Annie
	McCreadie, Karen.
Dewey Number:	381.14092

Cover design by Tess McCabe

Cover photo © Fairfax Photos/Marina Oliphant

Printed in China by Printplus Limited

10 9 8 7 6 5 4 3 2 1

Disclaimer
The material in this publication is of the nature of general comment only, and does not represent professional advice. It is not intended to provide specific guidance for particular circumstances and it should not be relied on as the basis for any decision to take action or not take action on any matter which it covers. Readers should obtain professional advice where appropriate, before making any such decision. To the maximum extent permitted by law, the authors and publisher disclaim all responsibility and liability to any person, arising directly or indirectly from any person taking or not taking action based upon the information in this publication.

Contents

Foreword

I have met so many people who have a story about my husband or a connection with Crazy John's, the company he founded. Sometimes it was just that they admired his style or his can-do attitude. People who had met him commented on how he always had time to stop and chat no matter how busy he was. There have been hundreds of people who have told me that their first ever mobile phone was a Crazy John's phone. I have also met many of the Crazy John's staff and they all had a story about John—both good and bad. When you share your life with a true achiever it's hard to fully comprehend the impact they can have on the broader community.

Unfortunately for my family, I learned about that impact the day John passed away. For those closest to him the world seemed to stand still that day, but later total strangers would tell me they will always remember where they were when they heard the news that John had died. At the age of forty-two John seemed to have so much ahead of him. His death reminds us of the need to grab what we can out of life and not stand back. My hope is that it also encourages more men to take the time to see their doctor for regular check-ups, to protect their families from grief.

Another health-related issue close to my heart, and that John was equally as passionate about, is the increasing number of children with food allergies. Our daughter Jaida was diagnosed with anaphylaxis to tree nuts, which led us to establish the Ilhan Food Allergy Foundation to support research into the causes of food allergies. To that end, sales of this book support the foundation, so it can continue its important work.

I trust John's journey gives hope to anyone with a burning desire to open a business or do something important in the community. John's story — a Muslim in a Western society who grew up in one of Melbourne's poorest suburbs and went on to become one of Australia's most successful entrepreneurs — proves anything is possible. That's what John always believed and it served him well. Be bold and have a strong belief and the possibilities are endless. I believe that will be John's lasting legacy. I hope you enjoy his story.

Patricia Ilhan
August 2009

About the authors

Stephen Dabkowski is a former business editor of *The Age*, having worked in the media for almost fifteen years for various publications including *The Sunday Age*, the *Herald Sun* and *The Herald*. Since leaving *The Age*, Stephen has taken up various directorships of not-for-profit organisations, including the role of CEO of the Ilhan Food Allergy Foundation. He also works as a communications consultant to various companies.

Annie Reid is a Melbourne-based writer. She has worked in the media for nine years, including four years in London, and now works as a freelance writer and communications specialist in Melbourne. Her writings have appeared in *The Australian*, the *Herald Sun*, *The Age*, Leader Community Newspapers and various property and lifestyle magazines. Annie also works with a number of corporate clients and non-government organisations. Annie can be contacted at <www.anniereid. com.au>.

About the contributor

Karen McCreadie is an author and professional ghost writer, specialising in nonfiction books. She has written seven books, including a specialist e-publication called *How to Write a Book in 33 Days: Develop Your Brand, Establish Yourself as an Expert, Protect Your IP and Make More Money Without the Struggle.* This book is aimed at those people seeking to create the ultimate business card—a book! Being an author creates powerful business development opportunities and can be an extremely efficient way to market a business. Karen has also co-authored a further three books and ghost written many more, including an international bestseller.

As a ghost writer Karen writes for CEOs, business coaches, consultants, international speakers, professional services personnel and entrepreneurs who have something worthwhile to share, but do not necessarily have the time or inclination to spend hours translating their ideas into a polished product. Recent titles have included topics as varied as wealth creation, personal development, change management and sports psychology. Thanks to modern technology, Karen works with clients in the UK, the US, Canada and Australia. For more information please visit <www.wordarchitect.com>.

Acknowledgements

This book would not have been possible without the support and guidance of Patricia Ilhan and John Ilhan's friends and family. The authors would also particularly like to thank Brendan Fleiter, Barry Hamilton and Ayse Ilhan for their assistance.

Stephen would like to thank his wife Mariella and children Gemma, Alexander and Zacharie for putting up with him during his absences to write the book, and his dog Zandrie for keeping him company during the late nights. He dedicates this book to his mum and dad who for him symbolise the story contained in this book about the merits of hard work and good values.

Annie would like to thank her family and close friends for their support during the writing of this book. In particular, she thanks Jayne, Bruce, Ross, Caroline and Paul, and her dog Nellie, for sitting under her desk so diligently. She dedicates this book to her grandfather, Geoff Taylor.

Preface

John Ilhan's dream was that one day every Australian would own a mobile phone. At the age of twenty-six, this simple dream fuelled the creation of his business, Crazy John's. This in turn led to John becoming one of Australia's most admired and successful self-made multimillionaires.

A Turkish migrant whose parents emigrated to Melbourne with just two suitcases, John's life is the quintessential rags-to-riches story. From his parents' bungalow in Broadmeadows to a multimillion-dollar beachfront home in Brighton, John attracted interest across the board and his public profile grew steadily as his business and philanthropic affairs escalated. In the meantime he married his wife Patricia and loved nothing more than spending time with his three daughters, Yasmin, Hannah and Jaida, and his son, Aydin. But John's life was tragically cut short in October 2007, when he suffered from heart failure during a morning walk along Brighton Beach. He was just forty-two years old.

Of course, John's story did not end there, and this book had even earlier beginnings. Karen McCreadie was originally commissioned by John Wiley & Sons in 2004 to write John

Ilhan's book. Karen conducted a series of interviews with John and wrote a manuscript called *The Black, the White and the Crazy*, as a reflection of John's business techniques and unique way of looking at the world. Although the book was successfully submitted to the publishers it was never published: John was in the middle of an epic court case with Telstra and wanted to delay publication until it was resolved. More importantly, John felt his story was far from finished. He believed he had only scratched the surface of his potential and wanted to wait until he had achieved more before publishing his story. Unfortunately the Telstra settlement took considerably longer than anyone had imagined and shortly after its conclusion John passed away.

In the months following John's death there were many loose ends to tie up. John's family and friends rallied to protect his many financial assets and philanthropic legacies. In addition, the many people whose lives had been touched in some way by John needed time to heal from their loss.

With so many aspects of John's life coming full circle towards the end of 2008, talk of completing the book re-surfaced. Public interest in John was still considerable—he had, after all, topped the *BRW* Young Rich List three years running—and it was clear that people wanted to read about his life and business. But it was Patricia's desire to tell his story publicly that saw the manuscript taken down from the shelf. Unfortunately Karen McCreadie was committed to other projects overseas at this time. Stephen Dabkowski, a former Fairfax journalist, speechwriter and communications consultant for both John and Patricia, was Chief Executive Officer of the Ilhan Food Allergy Foundation and was there-fore perfectly placed to bring the book up-to-date. A personal friend of the Ilhans, Steve was already familiar with much of John's story and Patricia trusted him to bring the project to fruition. He enlisted the help of a colleague, Annie Reid, a journalist and writer, to co-write the book, and for many months the two worked to reshape the manuscript with a biographical perspective.

As a result, this book has undergone its own journey. Importantly, John's presence is evident throughout, owing to the book's first version authored by Karen McCreadie, but the story could not have been told without the vital contribution of everyone involved. It is a great credit to the people around John that his story can now be shared, with the hope that his legacy will touch future generations.

Stephen Dabkowski and Annie Reid
Melbourne
August 2009

Chapter 1

Man of the people

26 October 2007

Peple came from everywhere, many of them never before having stepped foot inside a mosque. The streets were clogged and the police had to install traffic barriers. There were the rich and the poor, the celebrities and hundreds of humble people, who just came to pay their respects.

The Melbourne suburb of Broadmeadows, considered one of the city's most disadvantaged areas, had never seen anything like it. A mix of expensive imported cars with their in-built navigation systems, guiding them to streets they had never visited before, were hastily parked behind more modest family sedans outside the small houses in the streets that surround the Broadmeadows Mosque with its trademark white tower. The traffic jam meant many people abandoned their cars and set off on foot to make the service on time. Expensive dark Italian suits mixed easily alongside traditional Islamic dress as the throng massed, by now numbering more than 5000 as the time approached 11.00 am. Television helicopters hovered overhead, while on the ground reporters not used to covering a traditional Islamic service jostled to get what they thought would be the best vantage point.

In effect it was organised chaos with people headed in all directions, but they all had one unifying thought on their mind. They were all there to farewell the man they called Crazy John. John Ilhan had died on 23 October at the tender age of forty-two, and still no-one could quite believe it. The special unifying force that John created was well illustrated on the day of his Islamic Cenaze. It was the day he drew people from all walks of life together—from the people John grew up with who were still living in Broadmeadows to captains of industry, including former National Australia Bank boss Ahmed Fahour and Daniel Grollo of the Grocon building empire, both of whom marvelled at John's achievement of creating something from nothing.

Most people who knew Ahmed were used to seeing him in a business setting, but later he would openly cry out in anguish and weep at the gravesite in Fawkner Cemetery. Commenting later on the type of person John was, Ahmed said, 'John never forgot who he was, where he came from or the friends he made along the way'. Daniel was quietly solemn and would later admit that John's death had caused him to take stock of his own busy life. 'He proved it is possible to overcome insurmountable hurdles and rise to a great height', he said.

Earlier in the day staff from the Victorian Premier John Brumby's office had called organisers at the mosque from the coastal town of Lorne, almost two hours' drive away, where the Premier was attending a community cabinet meeting. They were trying to work out a way for him to fly back via helicopter to get to the funeral on time and were looking for landing sites. Unfortunately for Mr Brumby there just weren't enough minutes in the day, leaving him unable to get back in time to Broadmeadows for the funeral, so the plan was scrapped at the last minute.

The then Prime Minister John Howard could not attend the service, but sent John's local MP Andrew Robb as his representative. The previous year Mr Howard had sent John a handwritten Christmas card and photo, which Patricia, John's wife, has had framed.

In Turkey, newspapers were proclaiming John as the man of the people, and the country sent its ambassador from Canberra to Broadmeadows for the service.

Crazy John always had drawing power and could generate publicity in an instant, but on the day of his funeral he excelled himself. He attracted celebrities, including Eddie McGuire and Shane Warne, who loved his can-do attitude. Crazy John's Chief Executive Brendan Fleiter comments that John achieved more in his forty years than most people would in two lifetimes: 'What struck me the most was he was a migrant from Turkey who grew up in Broadmeadows and rose to a very senior position in our community. To my mind John lived until he was 100; he just did it in forty-two years.'

Cricket legend and friend Shane Warne recalls hearing the news John had passed away. 'I was in Melbourne ... I was driving around when I first heard the news on the radio', he says. 'I just couldn't believe it. Then my phone started ringing with people calling to tell me. I couldn't believe it happened on his morning walk. It was a really difficult time because I'd lost a friend, and I felt so bad for Patricia and the kids.'

John's close friend Eddie McGuire said, 'The thing that struck me about John when I first met him is what a nice guy he was. Maybe you thought he was a bit naive, but then you realised he knew what he was doing. I knew of his brother

Gerald, who was a legend around the northern suburbs in Melbourne, and I knew John was no knucklehead. The thing was he always stood by his word.'

John's funeral also drew loyal staff and customers of Crazy John's who just came to say thank you. Most noticeable were the hundreds of members of the Turkish community, many of whom had never met the man, who came to offer a personal appreciation of someone who symbolised so successfully the joining together of the Australian and Turkish communities.

Everyone had an eye out for John's family. His father Ali, looking ashen-faced, contemplating having to bury a second son, who died so young, at the same mosque. John's mother Nezaket might have been small in stature, but her inner strength was noticeable under her black hijab. Patricia arrived with her three daughters—Yasmin (then aged nine), Hannah (aged eight) and Jaida (aged six). Patricia's young son Aydin—just ten months old—was left at home with a babysitter as he was too young to attend. By Patricia's side was John's sister Ayse who has become the children's rock and a lasting connection to their father.

The limousine bringing the immediate family was led through the surging crowd at the mosque by the police. As the car door opened the crowd heaved, but Patricia did not seem to notice. Everything was a blur—like the past three days since the moment the police had knocked on her door to tell her the tragic news about John. For seventy-two hours everything had just been about getting things organised, arranging for John's parents to return from Turkey so that, under Islamic tradition, he could be buried within three days of death, and doing all she could to support the children. Patricia had also become used to receiving the hundreds of mourners at her home in Brighton, which became a virtual open house to all. After her initial disbelief at the size of the crowd, for the first time Patricia felt scared. She had never imagined such a crowd.

'I wasn't aware of the overall size of the crowd', she recalls. 'I think I saw later on the news that there were about five thousand people there and that was the first idea I had of how big it was. All I could think about was that the children were going to get crushed and all I wanted to do was protect the girls. I was concerned that one of them would get pushed away in the crowd. I saw a few people around me. I saw Eddie McGuire because he came up to me and I saw a few other people, but that's all. I wasn't really looking at the people.

'I couldn't stop thinking about our life together. It was ten years of marriage—almost eleven—and three years together before that. I was thinking about the birth of our four children and what we went through to have Aydin. I had three miscarriages before I had Aydin. I was reminiscing about what we'd achieved in such a short period of time. When I think back to when we first met—we were twenty-nine—we were just kids in the way we acted. I remembered us arguing over silly things and I look back to how far we progressed as people.'

Soon after arriving, Patricia and the children were ushered to the final viewing of the body in a room at the rear of the mosque, as per Islamic custom. The girls had been warned this would happen and stuck close to their mother.

'The actual viewing at the mosque was my second viewing of John,' Patricia says, 'because I'd already gone to the coroner's office to view the body with Ayse about thirty-six hours after he died. When I saw him the second time I actually thought he looked a lot better—there wasn't all the swelling around his face like when I saw him the first time, which was quite shocking. So when the children saw him it was good because they said he looked exactly like he was sleeping. Other than the memory of him waving goodbye for his fateful walk three days earlier, they had seen him so many times asleep on the couch at home. It was comforting to me that their last vision of him was that he did look like him when he was comfortable and asleep.'

During the Islamic service, all the prayers were in Arabic. John's sister Ayse translated for the children and Patricia.

When the body was placed in the hearse, Patricia and the girls got in the car immediately behind. The crowd began to part, but there was a wait of a few minutes before the funeral procession was able to move off. Patricia used those few minutes to remind the girls of who their dad had really been.

'The kids kept asking which car daddy was in. I showed them how the police had closed the road and that's because daddy was such an important man and he did so much for the community. A child wouldn't understand that they don't do this for everybody. They needed to be aware how this had affected the whole community and I don't think they realised that this situation at the funeral was not normal. I wanted them to look out of the window and realise that their daddy had achieved something amazing. Then I started thinking back to where it all began, which was appropriate because we were in Broadmeadows, where John grew up.'

A month later a public memorial service was held at the Melbourne Exhibition & Convention Centre, which was attended by the Premier, John Brumby, and more than 1000 mourners who came to pay their respects. Clearly, John Ilhan was a man who had touched thousands of lives.

Chapter 2

A better life

1939–1973

The story of John Ilhan—the boy from Broady who made it big—should never really have happened. The effort it took for his family to leave Turkey and come to Australia is an against-the-odds tale, and one that would be familiar to many families that immigrated to Australia in the 1960s and 1970s.

In addition, John's rags-to-riches business story might have only been possible in Melbourne. His assault on the mobile phone industry relied on Melbourne's immigrant communities, so it was fortunate that his father did some fast talking and convinced the Immigration Department to let the Ilhan family settle in Melbourne rather than New South Wales, which was their original destination.

John Ilhan should have grown up in Ankara in Turkey. He probably would have followed his grandfather's footsteps and opened a small business. In fact many of John's skills as a trader and salesman could be traced back to his grandfather

Bekir Ilhan, who ran a general store in Yozgat, in central Turkey, 200 kilometres east of Ankara. Bekir Ilhan travelled the countryside sourcing goods at the best possible price to sell in his store, while John's father Ali ran the store as a boy and young adult.

Ali was born on 20 December 1939. It was a simple, almost rural, life, but one that totally agreed with him. He was a handsome boy whose role running the general store placed him in a position of influence within the local community. 'I came from a small town outside of Ankara. I was considered the village boy when I came to Ankara to visit, but that had a number of advantages. I was good-looking and people were interested in me because I was not from Ankara', he says. It was this self-confidence that also became a trademark of Ali's children, but was best inherited by John.

It was on one of Ali's visits to Ankara that he met Nezaket (whose name means polite and gentle) at the house of a mutual friend. The two could not take their eyes off each other. At that time Ali was eighteen and Nezaket was only fifteen.

'I think I was handsome and I know I had every village girl chasing me, but Nezaket caught me. Her mother introduced us and soon after that we decided to marry. Her family wasn't thrilled that she was getting married so young, but it was what we decided to do', Ali recalls.

The pair married in 1960, but the newlyweds did not have much time to settle in to life together, as soon after their wedding Ali began two years of compulsory national service. Nezaket settled in Yozgat to wait for Ali, but suffered a tragic blow when she gave birth to a boy who died at three months old. His name was Ahmet, and no-one knew why he had died. Ali never got the chance to meet him because he was completing his military service and had decided not to take leave so that he could finish early and return home to his wife.

In 1962 Nezaket gave birth to a boy called Celal (pronounced Jelal) — who later became known as Gerald.

Once Ali completed his national service, and with a baby in tow, the family moved to Ankara. Ali recognised the importance of education (something he would later emphasise to his children) and enrolled to complete his high school certificate while working as registrar in the law faculty at Ankara University. Working at the university turned out to be a fateful decision for Ali, one that would help shape the Ilhan family's future. Ali's time at the university meant that he was at the forefront of both intellectual and radical thinking. He witnessed a number of student demonstrations and he began to hear about a military takeover to quash the uprisings that had been bubbling since 1960 when the first coup d'état in Turkey took place. At the time there were riots in the streets between the communists and anti-communists, and life for Turkey's citizens was dangerous.

'We knew a civil war was brewing. I worked in the legal library at Ankara University. I listened to the students and I knew there would be a military reaction. I wanted to look after my family', says Ali. His fears turned out to be correct. In 1971 Turkey suffered a 'Coup by Memorandum', which was followed in 1980 by a major coup headed by General Kenan Evren, Chief of the General Staff.

Despite the political unrest that was brewing, Ali and Nezaket settled into an enjoyable routine in Ankara. They had an apartment just a short walk from the university and Ali would return home each day at noon for lunch prepared by Nezaket. Ali would then have a short siesta. Today Nezaket jokes she would 'press his pants and shirt and make certain when he left for work again he was the best-looking man at the university'.

In Ankara the next major milestone for Ali and Nezaket was the birth of their second son, Mustafa, on 23 January 1965. Mustafa was physically smaller and fairer in skin colour (a fact that would have significance later) than Celal, and cheekier than his older brother. He would not be called Mustafa for long either. He would became known as John from about the age of seven when his primary school teacher at Pascoe Vale North Primary School in Melbourne, who could not pronounce his name, dubbed him John and the name stuck. The young Ilhan family continued to grow with the birth of John's sister Ayse (pronounced Aisha) in March 1967. However, in another cruel twist of fate, Nezaket fell pregnant again, but miscarried at six months.

'Apparently the child had died in the womb and the placenta was poisoning her', Ayse recalls. 'I remember very clearly at the age of [about] two playing in our yard in Ankara and looking for my mother. I found her lying on the ground with green stuff all over her. I called for my paternal grandmother who was living with us. An ambulance took her to hospital and the doctor said the placenta was poisoning her and she would have died if she had arrived at the hospital five minutes later. This child was also a boy.'

Now with three children to support and increasing signs of political instability in Turkey, Ali moved quickly to leave the country. He wanted to give his children the best start to life, and feared that living in Turkey would be too dangerous. 'The first destination we applied to go to was to Holland, but they had an immigration rule where only the parents were allowed to migrate first and the children were to follow two years later. But that would have split up the family and although we passed the medical examination and had every right to go, we decided against Holland', Ali says.

'A lot of our friends had put in an application to go to Australia, so we thought about that, even though we didn't know much about the country. We had friends who had migrated to Australia in 1968, and they had written a letter to us about Australia and sent us a newspaper. Suddenly, Nezaket wanted to go. We had to go to Istanbul to obtain the migration application, so we decided to go there as a family and get the application. We literally knew nothing about Australia.'

Ali and Nezaket made their first application to migrate to Australia in 1969. Ali was thirty-one years old and Nezaket was twenty-six. Their application was accepted one month later; the fast turnaround due to the fact that there was no waiting list. Australia was known to be rural and infested with snakes, so many people were wary about migrating there. The children were too young to comprehend how their lives were about to change and how they would have to leave everything behind in Turkey. The skilled migrant program in Australia was paid for and organised by the Australian government and required immigrants to work for two years in exchange for accommodation upon arrival.

Once the family had been approved for migration and had decided to go, they knew there would be a wait before they could move, so Ali enrolled in an English language course — a fateful decision that would pay significant dividends later. 'I felt that it was important that I spoke the language of the country I was going to. That's why I did the course', Ali says. They would have to wait ten months before they could move to their new country.

'We only took two suitcases of clothes with us on the plane to Australia, and we were just so grateful that the Australian government was able to arrange everything. We had an arrangement with friends [who were living in the inner-city Melbourne suburbs of] Brunswick and Carlton to help us when we first arrived. They said they would come and pick us up from the airport. That gave us hope that we would settle well', Nezaket recalls.

'The day we left for Australia with the three children there was much hope, after all, we had made the decision to leave for a better life. We really did start with nothing. That was all we arrived in Australia with.'

The journey on a chartered Qantas jet to Australia was long and exhausting. They left Ankara on 27 July 1971 and arrived in Australia on 29 July. Their flight, with around 300 people crammed into an ageing Boeing jet, went via Tehran, Karachi, Hong Kong and Jakarta, and finally to Sydney. For Ali and Nezaket there were the considerable worries of what lay ahead of them to contemplate during that three-day international trek — let alone the stress of three children under the age of eight constantly crawling over and under the seats throughout the long trip.

The flight the Ilhan family had boarded was primarily being used to ferry fit and able Turkish migrants to ready-made jobs at various factories in Wollongong. Ali had signed up for this but he did not want to go to Sydney, he wanted to go to Melbourne where he had friends. Being one of the few people on the flight who could speak English, Ali approached the immigration officials and asked if he and his family could catch a connecting TAA flight to Melbourne, instead.

Ali was clearly able to display the inner-salesman family trait that would serve John so well, and, of course, his English skills were a significant advantage. As a result, the immigration officials said yes. Others on the flight were amazed that Ali had been able to talk the officials into providing his family with an extra flight to Melbourne. 'Everyone else on the plane wanted me to also negotiate on their behalf to go to Melbourne, but that was not possible. I managed to talk the officials into us coming to Melbourne because I knew we had some friends there. I knew it would help us settle quicker as a family', says Ali.

That day the Ilhans took a different path thanks to some quick talking from Ali at 30000 feet en-route to Australia. No-one will ever know whether John's transformation to the mobile phone king would have been possible if the Ilhan family had been forced to go to Wollongong to begin their life in Australia working at a steel mill.

Of the 300 people on board that long flight from Turkey only one got quite sick—Mustafa Ilhan. 'John didn't like the airline food. He just wouldn't eat and for that reason he got quite sick. We were very afraid for his health, so after we arrived in Melbourne we took him to the doctor, but they couldn't find any medical reason why he wouldn't eat', Nezaket recalls.

For a while John flatly refused to eat anything, and Ali and Nezaket did not know how to find out what was causing this behaviour. They thought the best approach was to try to offer him different types of food to find out what he liked. 'Eventually we discovered he only liked two foods—tinned tuna and fetta cheese. That's what he lived on in those early days in Australia', says Nezaket. Luckily for John, the Greek community was already well established in Melbourne and there were plenty of markets selling European foods. Nezaket was able to buy John his fetta cheese, but it was not until he was seven or eight that he began trying other foods.

After arriving in Melbourne in mid 1971, the couple did not waste any time in getting their first jobs. Friends took Ali along to a factory in the northern suburb of Preston—the J Gadsden canning factory—and Ali was asked to work the night shift. His weekly wage was $46. Nezaket's first job was at a tile factory where she earned a weekly wage of $28.

The Ilhans initially stayed with friends before renting a house for $22 a week at 22 Greenwood Street, Pascoe Vale. They lived there for a year as they settled in to Melbourne. 'The landlord was a lovely young Greek man named Bill', recalls Ayse. 'He would visit us almost weekly and take all three children on outings to parks and buy us treats such as ice cream. My mother would describe him as a beautiful person who would virtually spend the entire rent on the children. This lovely man would later find us after all those years at [John's] first Brunswick store.'

While working at the canning factory Ali took every opportunity to increase his level of higher education. For three months he undertook an English language course at the Royal Melbourne Institute of Technology (RMIT) and was even offered a job at La Trobe University, but the money wasn't as lucrative as factory labour. Instead Ali stayed at the canning factory from 1971 to 1973. 'We couldn't afford to live off the wage I was being offered at a La Trobe, so I needed to work night shifts to save some money', he says. 'The work was very hard. It was twelve-hour shifts and you never stopped, but it was fine.'

In 1973 Ali had a change of career that would have a significant influence over John's employment prospects later in life—he got a job at the Ford Motor Company factory in Broadmeadows. Nezaket had worked for a few other factories before starting at Ford in 1972, on the factory's production assembly line. She is only a small woman, but that didn't stop her from taking on one of the most physical tasks—installing dashboards in Ford Falcon sedans. 'If it's an easy job, I don't like it', Nezaket says. She alerted Ali to job opportunities at the factory and Ali decided to leave the back-breaking night shift at the canning factory and join his wife working on the production assembly line.

Ali made a career at Ford, working for the company from 1973 to 1992. He began in the plastics plant and after two months was asked by the union to be the shop-floor steward. Once again his English language skills gave him a great advantage in the largely migrant workforce at Ford. 'When they elected me shop steward the union told others about me: "There's a man who looks like he knows what he can do". Suddenly I was elected', Ali recalls. He kept moving up the seniority scale at the car factory, and eventually he was offered the position of leading hand, or foreman, on his shift.

Ayse remembers helping her dad carry out the union business by making what, as a child, she believed were important trips to the big city. 'Dad would take me into the city and he would deliver papers to the union office. He would translate the information provided by the union from English to Turkish for the Turkish workers.'

It was not long before a strong and coordinated work pattern was established within the Ilhan household—Nezaket working the day shift at Ford and Ali working the afternoon shift. There was a two-hour gap where the two would cross paths in and out of their respective jobs. The parents hardly saw each other, and John and Ayse would be taken care of by Gerald, who they looked up to as a father figure, after school. All three children were aware of how hard their parents were working and would try to make their lives easier by doing chores around the house. Gerald would ensure that these jobs were done, so that Ali and Nezaket knew they could rely on him.

Despite the high price of housing, the Ilhans were determined to provide their children with a roof over their heads. 'I accepted all the overtime I could get my hands on and at the time I was earning $87 per week. I managed to pull together a deposit of $9000 and borrow the rest for the house', Ali says. Nezaket was earning around the same.

With two incomes Ali and Nezaket's desire to 'get ahead' and obtain financial independence began to be realised. The Ilhans bought the family's first home at 45 Hales Crescent in Jacana (a neighbouring suburb of Broadmeadows) in 1973 for $22 000. When it came time to move, however, the owners needed to extend the settlement date, so there was another three months' delay. In the meantime, the Ilhans moved into a block of flats in Albion Street, Brunswick.

As it turned out it was a very safe loan for the bank to agree to because within nine months Ali had paid off the mortgage. The couple worked double shifts almost every day to do so, which enabled them to not only pay off their mortgage quickly, but also ensure that their children never went without.

'My mother handled all of the finances and for many years my father didn't know how much he would bring home in his pay packet. In those days it was cash in a small yellow envelope, which he would leave for my mother on their dressing table', Ayse recalls.

'My parents worked extremely hard and long doing very hard labour building various parts of cars. They actually weren't aware they had paid off the mortgage until the bank notified them, telling them that not only was it paid off, but they were also in credit. So my parents announced that we were going shopping to buy our first colour television. The whole family got in the car and drove to a store called Northern Electronics, on Gaffney Street in Coburg. Dad said, "You kids pick—whatever you choose we will buy". It was a Swedish brand, Luxor. We were rapt!'

The house in Jacana would be the Ilhan family home from 1973 to 1993. Today the house looks like a tiny bungalow, but it was to the family's liking. There were three bedrooms—one bedroom for the two boys to share and another for Ayse. Later, as he grew older and more independent, Gerald would occupy a room out the back. 'My parents did a fantastic job settling in Australia. They were still relatively young when they left Turkey. There should have been hiccups but there weren't. Whatever they did, they did it for the family', says Ayse.

From there the Ilhans moved fifteen minutes north to a house at 48 Mitchell Cresent in Meadow Heights. But the Jacana house was the yardstick by which John measured his success and he always remembered it. Just a few months before he died, John was interviewed by the US-based Discovery Channel for a series it was putting together on successful business leaders. The series, which was viewed by around 400 million people, was called *Great Fortunes of the World*. John drove out to Jacana to show the film crew (and viewers) the humble house where his story began, drawing a crowd on his arrival, having driven there in his custom-built Bentley.

Ali and Nezaket continued to work hard—shiftwork and overtime at Ford were the norm—and save, putting deposits on two blocks of land for John and Gerald as an investment for their future, with a plan to do the same for Ayse. But it did not mean it was always all work and no fun in the Ilhan household. The family had a small car to get around in and they went on camping and picnic trips every year.

'We'd sometimes jump in the car with all the kids in the back and just drive. Sometimes we didn't even know where we were headed. We'd just drive often by ourselves or sometimes with other carloads of people. I remember we took off one time on the highway and ended up in South Australia', Ayse fondly recalls.

Looking back Ali says that under the terms of the immigration agreement he and his family were legally required to stay in Australia for two years—to leave any earlier would have resulted in them having to repay their travel costs. Those two years were Ali's hardest time in Australia, when he worked pressing tins in a hot metal factory. Always in the back of his mind was the thought that if things did not work out they could return to Turkey. Ayse today jokes about the dilemma that faced her father at the time: 'It was like a mobile phone plan, you signed up to a contract for twenty-four months and you had to stick to your contract.'

The hard labour eventually took a physical toll on Nezaket. In 1993 she suffered permanent injury to her neck and could no longer work. She was taken from Ford in an ambulance to a medical centre, where she was later told that tendons in her neck had been damaged.

But Ali is clear that despite the hard work he was determined to push on with a new life in Australia. 'At the end of that time [the first two years] there was never any discussion about going back to Turkey', he says. 'We were here to stay. We wanted to make a success here in Australia, but little did we know then how successful things would become or who would be the driving force.'

With Ali and Nezaket settled working for Ford, it was then time to focus on the children. But they could never have imagined how their children would evolve over the next decade, or who they would become.

Chapter 3

Becoming a man

1974–1983

As a boy one thing always ensured John stood apart: he always asked 'why'. He was never satisfied with the status quo. This trait showed itself from a young age. 'From the earliest age, John was a thinker and an observer. He talked, but he also listened', recalls his father Ali. 'John observed things differently. He wouldn't just play with a toy, he would dismantle it and see how it worked. He always wanted to understand how things worked.'

John's sister Ayse was always a willing follower, and enjoyed how he questioned and challenged everything that interested him. She remembers a loving and cheeky boy, but someone who ultimately liked taking the lead. 'My earliest memories of John are at our first home in Australia, in Pascoe Vale in Greenwood Street. We'd run around and he'd chase me and I'd hide behind Mum.'

'John had a great influence on me. I mean, I was just two years younger than him, so we were close. Gerald was the older brother and I always behaved well next to Gerald because we loved him and he helped look after us like a parent, whereas with John it was different and we used to muck around together', Ayse says.

'I did anything I could to grab his attention. I loved the things he loved and obviously that was a way to be his friend and vice versa. Going back to the age of four or five we played "Cowboys and Indians" and he chased me around the house.

'Another thing I recall is we'd sit on the couch to watch television in the old black-and-white days and he'd always make me get up and walk to the TV to change the channel. He'd stay on the couch and relax', Ayse laughs.

'He taught me a few things from the earliest days of my life—like music. The first band that I liked he loved, so he used to get me to sit there and listen to music and recite the lyrics. The band was The Sweet and they had a single that had "Fox on the Run" on one side and "Ballroom Blitz" on the other. We'd sit there and he'd stop the record player and quiz me on the lyrics and he'd play air guitar because he wanted to be a rocker. I grew to love the song because he loved it. This would have been [when I was in] grade two.'

Living in Pascoe Vale meant that the first school John attended was Pascoe Vale North Primary School. However, he transferred to Jacana Primary School at the age of nine, following the family's move to Jacana. Ayse believes that it was at Jacana Primary that John experienced his first bout of racism, but he refused to let it affect him.

'At school he was popular', she recalls. 'He was always good at making friends and a lot of kids wanted to be his friend. He wasn't the shy type to be held back. There was one teacher who I think resented that he was so popular. This was the teacher who John would always remember telling him in front of the class: "You won't amount to anything". I remember it as well because it was a composite grade five and six class, and I was in grade five and John was in grade six.

'The folding wall that separated our classrooms would be opened up and we would sit with each other. I remember this female teacher giving John a hard time, and looking back I think it had a great deal to do with racism. Of course we didn't know what it meant back then. I mean you have to remember that the three of us were the only Turkish kids at school, let alone Muslims. Overall the school was fantastic, there were just some individual teachers and students who gave us a hard time and we couldn't work out why we were being treated so differently.'

The incident in grade six where a teacher told John he would amount to nothing obviously stayed with him. In an interview with the ABC's *Catalyst* program in 2003 he recounted the school episode as being one of the most defining moments in his life, which encouraged him to fight back against authority and believe in himself: 'In the last couple of days of primary school—I was a bit shocked actually—I had a female teacher and she just pointed to me and said, "I'm not sure where you're going to end up young man". I didn't think I was such a bad kid.'

John went on to attend Broadmeadows Secondary Coll- ege, at the time one of the most disadvantaged government schools in Victoria, where he was fortunate to have teachers who encouraged him. He went back to his old school in 2006 as part of a documentary called *That Was Me*, developed by the Education Foundation to promote public education and screened on Channel Seven. There John was reunited with his favourite teacher John Solomon. In contrast to his experience in primary school, this teacher saw something special in John, and according to Ayse told John's parents at parent–teacher meetings, 'John can achieve anything he puts his mind to'.

Another teacher John remembered fondly was Richard Mills, his grade six teacher and basketball coach. Richard had a panel van and would drive around and pick up the kids — they would all pile in the back — and he would drive them to the games. '[Richard] put aside Saturdays to help out the kids. It was fantastic fun. Years later Richard's daughter sent John an email passing on Richard's regards and congratulating him on his success and that meant a lot to John', Ayse recalls.

Sport — or more particularly soccer — played an important role in the development of John's psyche and the self-confidence he displayed in later life when he started his own business. The story of how John ultimately came to play soccer at the highest levels is a study in youthful determination to succeed no matter the personal embarrassment.

Ayse remembers his drive and self-belief: '[He went] to soccer training three times a week, but he never talked about the actual games. It was only later, when John mentioned in some newspaper interviews that he was never actually given a game, when the memories actually began to clear in my mind. My parents and I used to go to watch Gerald play, and then wait around and hope John got a game. He was always on the bench. As a junior he never got a game.

'Just imagine it: he'd walk more than a kilometre to soccer training from our home three times a week, and walk to where the games were being played and he'd just sit on the bench. The key was he did not give up. He refused to believe he wasn't good enough; he had the self-belief to know he was good at soccer. John's daughter Hannah is like that at gymnastics, she is always trying harder to get it right. When it comes to that sort of thing it's almost like tunnel vision. John had that as a young man.'

Ultimately John did get a game at Broadmeadows City Soccer Club and went on to become captain of the team that initially rejected him. He was a fast and effective midfielder with a goal–scoring eye that quickly caught the attention of talent scouts in higher league teams. John's ultimate achievement was to play briefly in the then highest league in Australian soccer—the National Soccer League—before a knee injury ended his playing days at about the age of nineteen.

John always said that the injury, which gutted him at the time, was the kindest blow of all because it made him think about life after soccer. Otherwise, he believed, he would have always kept flirting with the idea that he could make it as a professional soccer player and not focused on developing a career and using his later evident business talents.

Overall, however, it was John's fixation with soccer that kept him out of trouble during his teenage years when many of his peers turned to other ways of keeping themselves occupied. John remembered the police coming to his high school to talk to the students about law and order, but the discussion descended into a joke about how many vacancies were left at Pentridge Prison for boys from Broady.

'As a young guy in Broadmeadows I didn't have the same opportunities as someone on the other side of the [Yarra] river', John told one newspaper interviewer. 'My wife is from Hawthorn—beautiful theatres, private school, ballets. What did we have? Great big paddocks and football [soccer]. Not much in the way of opportunities.

'I don't know why but I had a lot more drive than a lot of my mates. A lot of them were too busy just bumming around. Years later I heard many them are in jail. Sport saved me, I would say, in more ways than one. If it wasn't for soccer, I would have been bumming around with them.'[1]

Ali remembers an important turning point in John's life when he began treating his two boys as adults and expected responsibility in return. 'I remember when Gerald was fifteen and John was thirteen, I took them for a drive to a quiet reserve and spoke to them both about the future. My view with children is that from birth to the age of seven you are a parent to a child. From the ages seven to fourteen as a parent you are their teacher, and from the age of fourteen onwards your child becomes your friend', Ali says.

'The speech went something like this: "Now you are both grown-up men, we are always going to act as a family. I will now ask your opinion and we will be friends. I now own my house, so if anything happened to me we have no relatives in Australia, but the house will be yours. You should take comfort in that".

'The reason for the speech was to teach them about responsibility. I wanted them to trust me, to always come to me if they had a problem. I never wanted my children to become distant from me. I knew at that point at least I could offer my two sons a roof over their head.

'I told them if there is anything I have learnt in life it is to love people. If you do they will love you back. Living life is all about respecting yourself and others — otherwise you will be the loneliest person in the world.'

John took this message on board. Today in every Crazy John's store there is a sign for staff that says: 'People only buy from people they like'. This was one of John's key selling tools and was passed on to staff during their orientation.

Ali noticed early on that there were great differences between his two sons. 'I told John when he wanted to do something as he got older that I would help him. But I also knew he would always think things through and that he was always on the right track. I trusted him that way', Ali says.

'His older brother, Gerald, was different. When he wanted to do something his first actions were always physical, he would act sometimes without thinking. Of course Gerald had other things to cope with. His dark skin meant he received a lot of unwanted attention, but he was always family oriented and looked after the other children when I wasn't there.'

The unwanted attention was spilling onto the school grounds, with Gerald often coming home with bruises and wounds from getting picked on and being involved in fights. It was enough to prompt Ali to go to the school and challenge the principal to act, but it was all brushed under the carpet.

Gerald's darker skin and the necessity for him to often play the protective parental role in his parents' absence led him into a world where he learnt self-defence. He would later become a Commonwealth kickboxing champion.

It was through Gerald that John met his best friend, Seb Pir. Like the Ilhans, Seb was Turkish and had emigrated to Melbourne, although not until he was twenty-seven. Seb was five years older than John and lived not far from him in Meadow Heights.

At the time in 1988, one year after Seb had arrived in Australia, he had had more in common with Gerald than he did with John, and this was mainly because he and Gerald were closer in age. Seb had become friendly with Gerald through kickboxing, and enjoyed watching his matches. He had also seen Gerald and John playing soccer, and at one stage the three boys played on the same team.

Seb was already married and his wife, Sam, enjoyed going along to the boys' games with her sister—even though they were the only girls on the sidelines. She formed an early opinion of John: 'John was more of the quiet type at soccer. We used to go up to Gerald and say, "Right, Gerald. Why's your brother such a snob? Why's he stuck up? Is he scared of girls?" Gerald would say, "No, my brother's a bit shy". John just kept more to himself.' As quiet as he was, his inner drive was expressed on the soccer pitch.

∽∾

One of the most famous stories about John's childhood was the day he told his mother, as a teenager: 'My first car is going to be a Porsche and I'm going to buy a house by the beach. I will look after you and dad well.' This story has been repeated in many newspapers since he became a household name, but according to Ayse, this statement wasn't about accumulating money or wealth, it was about John giving back to the people he loved.

'John didn't actually care about the money, it was about what it could buy, what opportunities you could create with that wealth. He wanted to look after his family first, especially Mum and Dad. Later it became about philanthropy and establishing the Ilhan Food Allergy Foundation', she says.

'I mean when John was first contacted by *BRW* for inclusion in the magazine's Young Rich List he didn't know how much he was worth and he was surprised anyone would want to know.

'We used to get pocket money when we were growing up and I never spent mine, and he'd always come and ask for some, which I'd give him. Later on, it might be a few weeks later, he'd give the money back to me, but he always gave me more than I gave him.'

John's mother Nezaket remembers him winning a large bet on a horse race when he was about eighteen. It was a $2 bet—a tip from a friend—and he won $1000. Still, he knew he shouldn't be gambling, so when he got home he started giving the money away to friends of his parents who were at the house. It was his way of softening the blow of being so successful—and dealing with the guilt of being wealthy in an unaccustomed way. John always felt better if he gave to others before giving himself anything.

Ayse recalls that as John neared adulthood he quickly embraced the family responsibility his father had spoken about to him and his brother. 'As we grew up, John and Gerald were my best friends and we would always stick together. They both guided me. For example, if John didn't approve of me going to a place for a party, he always reminded me that I was a lady and some places were not suitable for ladies. How I dressed and behaved was all a result of the confidence and influence afforded to me by John and Gerald. A peer group didn't exist for me—my confidence and strength came from both my brothers, and them making the time to explain everything to me. Whatever it was—I would speak to John about everything.'

John did not have a part-time job while he was at high school, but Ayse remembers how differently he thought from the other students when it came to organising a work experience placement in year ten. 'When he had to go out and find a job for work experience, John just said, "What am I going to do? It's not as if what I find is going to be my career". His whole attitude was something bigger. Anyway, he ended up going to some agency and he got offered to do modelling for a Kmart catalogue. But he didn't know it was modelling underwear, so he went there and they said, "Okay, try these on", and John said, "I thought I was going to wear clothes", and they said, "No, underwear". He said, "I'm not doing that", and walked out.'

As John grew older something else happened. Forged by his growing self-confidence and success on the soccer field, his grades at high school improved and after completing year twelve at Broadmeadows Secondary College he was accepted into an arts degree at La Trobe University. John was just one of a handful from his graduating class who would pursue tertiary education, which made his parents particularly proud.

With his father having worked at a university in Ankara, Ali knew the importance of education and wanted John to obtain a university degree. In Turkey the extended Ilhan family was well educated, working in parliament and the defence force, as engineers and in other specialised professions. Ali wanted John to do the same.

'Academically he was good at school, but he was a bit overwhelmed at university. He didn't like the fact that he was being encouraged to participate politically at uni.[2] John wanted to study—maybe he also chose the wrong subjects', says Ayse.

In the end John lasted just one year at La Trobe, much to the displeasure of his parents. 'At first he wanted to defer uni, work a while, save some money and buy a car, and then go back. That's what he told my parents, but they were devastated. They wanted him to continue with university, but the salesman inside John wanted to get going, and when John decided to do something you couldn't stop him', Ayse recalls.

John later admitted in an interview that formal education was not for him. 'If you want to be really, really successful, I just think maybe [learning to be] streetwise is important. That means to understand people and not manipulate people—make them understand your vision, your dream, and find out how you get them to believe in the same thing and really put in [work hard] and really care. I think that's probably understanding people.'[3] John preferred another form of education—learning on his feet. It was the entrepreneur in him beginning to emerge.

Friends believe this was why John was always going to be his own boss, and why the proven route to success—via the best schools or university or the old school ties—was not for him. Taking the unorthodox path—and forgetting the status quo—was John's way of continuously moving forward.

Chapter 4

Understanding business

1984–1990

It was fortunate for the Australian telecommunications ind- ustry that university life bored John. The real world was far more exciting, and he was bursting with desire to get out there and start making a name for himself.

In 1984, at the age of nineteen, John heard about a job that was on offer at Ford Motor Company's head office, in its Ford Credit department. Fuelled by grand dreams of wearing a suit every day and working in a corporate environment, he applied for the job. However, it was in vain—John was told the company was only considering internal candidates. As his sister Ayse recalls: 'He thought, "Okay, why don't I get a job at Ford and then re-apply?" Back then it was easy to get a job on the production line, so that's what he did.'

When he made the announcement to Ali and Nezaket that he would soon be starting at Ford on the production assembly line, they were mortified. 'They said we work here because we've got no alternative, but you do. John said, "Just watch me. I'm going to get that job in the office in two weeks—you'll see. I'm going to come to work in a suit"', says Ayse.

John spent one week fitting batteries into cars and another adding door trims at Ford and tired quickly of the monotonous nature of production line work. But then a stroke of luck hit when a junior position became available at Ford's head office. John applied immediately and got the job. He could leave the factory floor and fulfil his dream of wearing a suit to work.

Not only would the job be John's first sales role, but he would also find that he and his new boss, George Stefanou, had quite a bit in common. Like John, George had experienced his own struggles growing up in a migrant family, and both men were very close to their parents. George had also tired of university life, dropping out of his humanities degree at Monash University after a year. They both loved soccer and played on different teams in the same league, sometimes against each other.

George grew up in the western Melbourne suburb of Avondale Heights and came from a strong Greek family. Not only was his father one of the first immigrants to work for Ford in the early 1960s, he also ran panel shops and service stations, and was able to pass on some of his car knowledge to his son.

George had joined Ford at the age of twenty, and like John it was also his first job. George was a few months older than John. 'At the time I was a car jockey. I moved all of the ex-Ford Motor Company cars from the national depot in Campbellfield, corralled them into one area and prepared them for sale. When I moved on, I had to have somebody replace me. Between myself and the chap who was the manager at the time, we advertised the job and the person that was selected was John Ilhan', George recalls.

John's new role supporting George was in junior sales. Incidentally, George was initially hired for John's job through the Commonwealth Employment Service (CES), which would later serve John well when it came to employing his own staff. 'John was a pretty shy sort of young bloke. He was certainly very family oriented and through the job he was able to not only be taught, but brought to the table his own ethics.'

Essentially, John was in charge of all of Ford's ex-company executive driven cars. He would list these cars for sale, organise their roadworthy certificates, service and clean them, and present the cars for viewing by the staff or dealers who were interested in purchasing them. It proved a very profitable way for Ford to clear out its used car fleet. At the time the company car fleet was part of the dealer development portfolio, and the Ford fleet typically represented about 3000 cars. It had to be turned over every nine months, so anywhere in the order of 12 000 cars were moved every year. With most of Ford's business in Melbourne the role involved plenty of responsibility.

'His typical day involved a fair amount of driving to and from head office to what was called the service garage. The service garage out at Ford Motor Company might only be 400 metres down the road, but it wasn't something that you necessarily walked to every day because you just couldn't. You were forever going backward and forward in cars', George says.

Although he was shy when he started, John was always well groomed and punctual. George remembers, 'He needed a little bit of attention to detail early on but ... you only had to say it once, twice at the worst and it was done, and he never went backwards'.

In a short time, John was proving himself and he and George were getting along superbly. Compared with installing batteries and door trims on the factory floor, this was definitely a move in the right direction. He was good at sales, people liked him and he liked people. He would make people laugh and customers enjoyed being around him.

'We absolutely loved and enjoyed everything we did, including things like playing soccer against one another', George recalls. 'We were both playing soccer at the time for different teams and enjoyed comparing notes and taking the micky out of one another on the field when we did play against one another.'

People thought their Turkish and Greek backgrounds would have caused some rivalry or bad blood, but it was exactly the opposite—they would often be mistaken for brothers. They got a lot of laughs out of the constant mix-ups, which extended not only to customers, but also staff at Ford.

Back then at Ford the cars were purchased using a special scheme, which placed John and George firmly in the spotlight. The cars were offered to staff first with the remainder offered to Ford dealer networks, which could be bought in closed tenders to the highest price. The price could be flexible depending on how long the staff member had been employed or the date they had last purchased a car.

'So everybody thought that they could get on side of you and maybe manipulate your area in terms of trying to get a car. Everybody basically wanted to know both of us as opposed to us needing to know everybody', George says.

As it transpired, the rules were being bent long before George and John came along, courtesy of a predecessor who had established a reputation for working under the radar. While their predecessor's fate was sealed with a stint behind bars, the boys still found themselves continually having their ethics tested.

But they were made of sterner stuff, as George recalls. 'It was important that we were beyond reproach in terms of what we could do because of the high-profile nature that it had. So that was something that we very, very much prided ourselves on, to the point where, when we didn't bend for one or two dealers on a specific thing, we were actually accused of not playing the game fair. It wasn't until we explained to their management what we were being asked to do that we were given full support as to the reasons we didn't do it.'

Another issue was red tape. George told John, 'If there was a job to be done, don't worry about getting four forms signed—just do it'. John was lucky that George and his boss were fully supportive of their staff as long as they were informed about what they were doing. It gave John an early taste for solving problems quickly as they arose.

The two would often reverse roles as well. John would step into George's administrative shoes while George would move the cars. When there was a downturn in the market, the boys would come up with creative ways in which to sell the cars, and they would play around with how much to put prices up or down and how often.

But there were times when they had to toe the company line, too, and George recalls passing on advice to John his father had taught him: 'I said, "Sometimes you're going to see some things here and you and I will look at one another and say, that isn't right. If you're not overly happy about it, express your opinion. Don't be afraid to express your opinion, but just make sure you've got something to back it up with".'

The strategy worked, and in a short amount of time their results were impressive. 'The first couple of years that we were together we were actually recording some of the best results we'd had at the time, in terms of not only selling those cars but selling them for more than their reserves', George says.

In 1987 George was promoted to a marketing position at the regional office. John was overlooked for the position George had vacated, partly because he didn't have a degree, but more so because a large number of graduates happened to be coming through the system when George moved on. What John did have was a dynamic personality and strong selling skills, but it didn't equate to a tertiary education.

In Ford's world, layers of management and bureaucracy thwarted creativity and innovation, and what was left was entrenched with policy and procedure. Again and again John was overlooked, with university graduates being picked for roles he knew he was qualified for.

Ayse recalls his frustrations when he saw so many new starters being promoted above him. 'His manager at the time had said something about being good enough, but he was always overlooked. Years later he ran into this man, who still works for Ford, at the football, who introduced himself while they were at a corporate box. John reminded him of what he had said and this man went red and was mortified.'

John believed there had to be somewhere that would reward hard work and entrepreneurial spirit. Somewhere he could set his own agenda and work without the harsh rigor of a bureaucratic company. He had spent three years at Ford, and he was ready for a change.

In 1987 a friend of John's — Steve — was working for a company called Strathfield Car Radio, a specialist, and then market leader, in the burgeoning telecommunications industry. It was a brave new world and the more John read and heard about it, the more he realised that it could be the ideal opportunity for him to really develop his sales skills.

Through Steve, he was invited to join the team at one of the Strathfield offices in Clarendon Street, South Melbourne. Little did he or anyone else realise that John would not only succeed in his career in telecommunications, but ultimately shape the entire industry.

Back then, however, it was very early days. On 23 February 1987 Telstra launched its MobileNet service. About $10 million was invested in developing the industry to make mobile communication possible, and Telstra pledged mobile coverage for eighty per cent of Australians.

MobileNet comprised about 500 radio base stations throughout Australia, with most covering a radius of fifteen kilometres. In the city areas the base stations were closer together to handle more users. The system worked by the base station receiving a message from a cellular phone, which was then connected to a switching computer before connecting the call. If you moved out of the radius of one base station, your telephone was automatically handed over to another radio base station with a stronger signal.

Telstra's first products comprised four models — the Explorer, the Traveller, the Attache, and the Walkabout. Costing several thousand dollars, the Walkabout was the most expensive and offered up to one hour of calls between recharges. Compared with the sleek, pocket-sized versions of today, the late-1980s models were heavy, clunky and unattractive.

By the end of 1988 Telstra had 31 500 portable phones connected to its network, with the phones retailing for up to $5400. Leading the pack were Strathfield Car Radio, Mobiletronics and Century 21 Telecommunications. John had seemingly chosen a great new career with the backing of a successful company.

John loved the dynamic nature of the phone business, and eagerly threw himself into his new role. He took up where he had left off at Ford, endearing customers quickly with his natural communication skills and willingness to listen to their concerns. Often the first to arrive at the shop and the last to leave, his down-to-earth manner was a godsend in a technical market, and customers were relieved to hear him untangle and simplify the confusing jargon.

Finally he was with a company that rewarded hard work regardless of qualifications, and to top it off, there was a sales incentive scheme, so he could work towards achieving both store and personal goals. Of course, he invariably qualified for the bonuses because clients were referring him to their friends and he was receiving multiple repeat sales.

Strathfield was keen to cement itself as a serious player in the industry and, recognising the importance of brand presence, decided to open a second store in 1990 in Sydney Road, Brunswick. There was just one problem. Not long after the store opened, the customers were not buying, and not only were they not buying, but the store was quickly losing its justification for existence.

Always one to keep an ear to the ground, John found out about the woes of the Brunswick store on the corporate grapevine. Quick as a flash, he raised his hand and asked if he could manage the store himself. The fact that the store was a lot closer to his home in Jacana meant that he wouldn't need to battle the city traffic each day. It was a convenient step up for him too; he knew the business and he was making consistent sales in his present job. But most importantly, it represented a challenge. John never did anything that wasn't hard, and this was certainly another level higher.

He was put on a trial as the manager of the Brunswick store. Staff were on either a morning or an afternoon shift, where the morning shift involved working in the store and the afternoon was spent on the road, or vice versa. Key to his approach was talking to the public, and John would walk onto building sites and around Brunswick chatting and telling people about the shop and what deals were on offer.

'It wasn't difficult. I got good people to work with me. I would build relationships with people, so they would see me around and we would become friendly. Because of the price of the phones in those days I thought you had to educate people about them. I remember an NEC 9B that was $5500 and yet I had sold a hundred of those to one customer. It wasn't about sales in the sense of opening a shop and waiting for people to come in. I was active in going out to the public and making sure they knew what was available. I'd take all the confusion away and open their minds up to the advantages of having a mobile phone — especially in businesses because that was the main market. I concentrated on certain businesses like construction. It was easy for them to understand the benefits and see the benefits on the bottom line by having their guys on the site and the foreman all connected by mobile phone. Sure, $5500 was a lot of money for a phone, but the value and time and manpower savings of being able to keep in touch with the site foreman and crew was bigger than that', John recalled.

'I also started to advertise in the local paper so that I would get even more recognition in the area. Once I built up a name, people trusted that I knew what I was talking about and I wouldn't bamboozle them. I was making about $5000 commission in a month. Mind you, it wasn't until later on that I realised how much the dealer was making. On that 100 phone order, for example, the dealer would have made something like a $70 000 margin. Not many of the other store managers were being as proactive as I was.'

Not one to rest on his laurels, John stepped back and looked at the bigger picture. 'When I look back on the decisions I've made in my life it's easy to see the junctions, those pivotal moments that changed the future. For me, the first one was managing the Brunswick store. I had no management experience, but I knew how to sell and taking that chance was the first step. Once I had proven I could manage a store and make it profitable I knew that there was no limit to what I could do!'

In three months John turned the Brunswick store from the worst-performing in the chain to the best-performing store in Victoria. Every month he was coming home with plaques and topping the sales list, selling three times more than his counterpart on the next rung up. Strathfield's biggest gesture was rewarding John with a Honda Prelude complete with leather interior.

However, Strathfield's well-intended incentive scheme was not so well structured. When it came to payout time, John found himself arguing about an overdue bonus of $1100 from the previous six months. Despite all his hard work at the Brunswick store and the profit he had generated, Strathfield still held out on paying him. He found himself once again angry and frustrated with his employer—simply as a matter of principle. He knew he was right, and couldn't tolerate bad management practices. John told Ayse, 'If I'm going to work so hard, I might as well work for myself'. So at the age of twenty-six, he quit.

Chapter 5

Going mobile

1991–1992

The timing could have been better. It was the height of the 1991 economic recession and Victoria was practically bankrupt. The repercussions of the June 1990 Pyramid Building Society collapse were still being felt in the wallets of the average Victorian, and John was feeling his own frustrations, too. Despite turning the Brunswick store from the worst to the best performing in the Victorian chain, he was smarting with the injustice of Strathfield Car Radio's refusal to pay his $1100 bonus owed from six months earlier.

John was now twenty-six, jobless and living at home in a self-contained bungalow at the bottom of his parents' garden. While many people in his position would have stewed and pondered their next move, enjoying a peaceful respite between jobs, this was not John's style. In fact, he had already made the move to launch into the next phase of his life.

It had been four years since Telstra had launched its MobileNet telecommunications service. Since 1987 more than 300 000 people had joined the network and business was booming. Telstra was confidently predicting that by the end of the century sixty per cent of all telephone calls would be either made or received by a mobile phone. In a relatively short time, mobile telephones had captured the imaginations of technophiles around the world. In 1991 the estimated total number of users of mobile phones worldwide was thirteen million. In 2008 this figure soared to over 3.3 billion.[1] It was a colossal industry with plenty of money seemingly up for grabs.

However, in Australia in 1991 subscribers were still mainly businesspeople or wealthy individuals. Priced at about $5400, mobile phones were too expensive for the average Australian. In addition, Telstra enjoyed a monopoly on the telecommunications market. Until August 1991, if you wanted a mobile phone, you had no choice but to connect to Telstra's MobileNet. John was convinced this was going to change and that he could make it work.

John wanted to be the best and he wanted the world to know who he was. He enjoyed sales and knew he was good at it, and he enjoyed helping customers make the best choice for their needs. He considered the possibility of working in a different field, but the temptation to seek revenge against Strathfield proved too great. He now had management skills and had proven to himself that he could make a business profitable. He saw his options as either getting a job with a competitor, or branching out on his own and going into business.

The decision was made for him when he saw that a shop in Sydney Road, Brunswick, directly opposite his former employer Strathfield, had recently become available. It was the perfect opportunity.

Sydney Road is a bustling urban streetscape. Home to a great variety of multicultural communities, it is a melting pot teeming with a rich religious, culinary and cultural fabric. Over the years many immigrants have added their own flavour to the road, creating new social venues, businesses and restaurants, and the vibrant strip has avoided the demise of other shopping strips with the development and expansion of shopping centres.

Not only would the location enable him to sink the boot into his former employer, but he could gain a marketing edge as well. Strathfield was splashing cash on brand development and advertising, so customers going into Strathfield on the strength of its advertising might look over the road and see his shop. Knowing full well that customers enjoy comparing prices and products, John believed they might be tempted to come in and take a look at what was on offer in his shop.

The strategy had worked well for Hungry Jack's over the years. One of its strongest marketing policies was to open an outlet near its main competitor, McDonald's. By offering people a choice, would-be McDonald's customers might change their minds and instead stroll next door to Hungry Jack's. John thought that he too could benefit from a similar arrangement.

Ever the entrepreneur, John decided that the shop idea was looking viable. His naive bravado told him that if he could make a store successful as manager, he could do the same as its owner. And so, straight after he handed in his resignation at Strathfield, John signed a lease to set up his first shop as owner and manager. Mobileworld Communications was born.

John walked into his brand-new business armed with only a few thousand dollars from his savings and little else. He recruited some mates to help with refurbishing, and the new premises was fitted out on a shoestring. He bought second-hand carpet from a local auction, another few friends built him a counter, and everyone pitched in to paint the walls. The first forays of Mobileworld were pretty basic.

John's parents' support was vital in the establishment of his new venture. Ali recalls John 'Came to me and said, "I want to start by myself. I was always salesman of the month or year at Strathfield, but I know I can be successful on my own". So I lent him $1500 to help him pay the bond and first month's rent on the shop, and after that I paid the $500 rent. I said to him, just give the business twelve months.'

Originally, Mobileworld Communications was to be opened as a partnership between John and another ex-employee of Strathfield Car Radio. John recalled, 'I was the phone manager and he ran the car radio division. So when I was talking about starting the business he said he wanted to come too and he would run the car radio side of things.

'Each of us registered as directors of the business. The carpet hadn't even been fitted when he told me he wasn't going to continue. It turned out he only wanted to be involved so he could show the paperwork to his bank manager and get a home loan.'

However, it was just a blip on the grand plan. As far as John saw it, the telecommunications industry was in great shape and offered solid potential, and he wanted his share. In addition, the recession was actually creating a marketing advantage for the main players. As businesses continued to operate more productively and efficiently, mobile phones began to be seen as a solution in markets where a high level of contactability was required, such as by contractors, sales professionals, construction companies and couriers. Mobile phones offered maximum efficiency, which offset the high costs.

But John was nowhere near being a main player. He was a nobody to Telstra, and his two-bit shop was miles behind his competitors. Unlike his larger competitors, he did not have a dealer agreement where he could receive commissions for connecting his customers to Telstra's MobileNet. The only way he could become a dealer was if Telstra could see there was potential in his business. As a start-up, John's potential was nonexistent, so he was on his own.

In those early days, the business operated on two streams of income—he could offer customers a new phone or sell second-hand handsets. The only issue was that he did not actually have any stock in his shop because he could not afford it. Unlike Strathfield, he did not have the luxury of distributors knocking at his door to provide phones, so he had to sell products directly from a brochure, which Ayse designed for him. She also created a brochure for a mail-out and made up flyers that they would photocopy at the local library. The flyers would then be slipped under Sydney Road shopkeepers' doors or handed out by John as he traipsed up and down the street.

To sell new stock, the process required great skill. As John was not a Telstra dealer, he was unable to actually connect customers to the Telstra MobileNet network, so he needed to convince customers to buy the handset from him instead of anyone else, even though he couldn't connect them. Until 1991 if you wanted a mobile phone you had no option but to connect to MobileNet. There were therefore no incentives for dealers and the only revenue was generated through hardware sales.

John had to convince customers to buy from the brochure and leave a deposit. He would then race over to the manufacturer and collect the phone, use the deposit to pay for it, and then deliver it to the customer. The customer thought this was great, not realising the service was actually born out of necessity. By delivering the phone, John received the rest of the payment and was then able to buy some more phones for the customer.

There were other more compounding issues: no signage and no marketing. Managing a store behind a recognisable brand is vastly different from working as a sole operator. Without employees, head office support and marketing muscle, any business is certain to struggle. In the marketing–led, price–led mobile communications business, marketing clout and distribution efficiency is crucial. John had neither.

As John recalled, times were hard. 'It was a pretty bleak time. I would be delivering these brochures and my friends would drive past calling for me to come to a club. I never went. I know they thought I was an idiot, but I was determined to make it work. It was much harder than I thought it would be and I was certainly forced to evaluate my decision more than a few times.'

The days were long. There was no differentiation between weekdays and weekends, and John was in the shop seven days a week, all day and most of the night, too. He believed that a physical presence in the shop was important, and even though there were no customers, it sent a message that Mobileworld was a viable business. On some occasions he slept overnight in the store on the floor.

The icing on the cake was a work function John attended during the first year of operation. It was a Telstra event held at the Hilton Hotel in Melbourne. Seeing the potential for networking, John thought it would be a great opportunity to promote his name and business in the industry. After donning his best suit and tie he turned up at the hotel and found the desk to register his name. He was told that he was not on the guest list and apparently there was no seat for him, either. It looked like Telstra was only interested in the big players and John was seen as more of a nuisance than an asset.

But John stood his ground. Despite feeling humiliated, he insisted that he be allowed to attend. Telstra relented and accommodated him. He recalled, 'No-one took me seriously in those days and it hurt, but at the same time it was the perfect motivation for me because I just got angry and it just made me even more determined to show them I was here to stay and I was a serious player in the market.'

In terms of sales, things weren't looking good either. In ten months the only thing he had sold was a second-hand pager worth $50. He had given that $50 note to his parents. By 1992 it was clear that the company was in deep financial trouble. In addition, John had accumulated a debt on his parents' home of $15 000. He couldn't obtain credit from suppliers or manufacturers, and his friends were making fun of his 'business'. The initial rush of enthusiasm had well and truly disappeared.

John's family continued supporting him without question, as Ayse recalls. 'Dad paid the mortgage and all of John's expenses — rent, utilities, stationery, "pocket money", etcetera — for whatever he needed, while friends helped with anything the shop needed, carpentry for shelving and desks. Gerald and I continued to work in our jobs to pay for the household expenses and we all made our vehicles accessible for John to use, particularly at night so that he could de-stress and continue with what was left of his social and personal life.'

But the debt continued to increase and the revenue was going in quite the opposite direction. Ali and Nezaket had sacrificed so much to provide for their three children, so John wanted to repay them before he had to confront the possibility that he might have to close the business. Just as Ali had worked tirelessly to provide a better life for his family, John was a fiercely proud man and couldn't give up.

'There was a period where I was soul-searching. I didn't want to be someone who gave up or was laughed at because I knew in the future people would not respect me. I would be looked at as a failure. Where would my credibility be? These things gave me the strength to continue', John said.

Not one for admitting defeat John hatched a plan. He approached his former employer Strathfield Car Radio and requested a meeting, simply saying he wanted to make them an offer. Not wanting to miss an opportunity to gloat over Mobileworld's seemingly imminent demise, Strathfield sent over a representative the following week. When asked what he wanted for the business John replied, '$15 000'. The rep looked shocked and waved his arms mockingly around the shop. 'But there's nothing here. You've got a phone line and a few brochures. I'll give you $5000.'

Another competitor, Mobiletronics, heard about John's financial troubles and that Strathfield was going to make him an offer. So it counter-offered, but interestingly only offered the same amount—$5000.

Looking back, John said, 'It was a good thing I think because I started to wonder if [Strathfield and Mobiletronics] were in cahoots, and that just made me mad. I never knew if they were, but it just made me even more determined to succeed.'

He would still have been $10 000 short had he accepted either of the offers and admitted it would have taken him decades to pay it off. He decided to approach a friend who had also worked at Strathfield and had left to go into business with his father in a bottle shop. Hoping to spark his attention, John proposed that Rob put in $7500 and come into business with him. His logic was that he would be able to turn the business around with the extra capital injection, but his mate declined. 'Things were really bad, they were just not working.

I was working until 12 am sitting alone. Even my girlfriend at the time left me because she thought I was a loser', John said.

After ten months, with just the one sale of the second-hand pager, there was still no improvement or growth, or indeed any indication that the business was heading upwards. It was at this point John realised his enthusiasm and blind hope were not enough. He could not rely on optimism and a positive attitude to propel him to instant business success, and the cold hard truth came as somewhat of a shock.

The business was disastrous and, by his own admission, John considered his persistence to continue delusional. He also struggled knowing that his failing business was being funded through an overdraft on the family home, but he was paralysed with confusion as to how he could make it all work. He decided he was ready to admit defeat and close the business. 'One Saturday, I went into the shop in my tracksuit—no suit—and starting whipping down the posters. I decided I was shutting up shop.'

He finally plucked up the courage to tell his father that he was going to have to close the business, and his mother Nezaket told her husband it was time for a father-and-son chat. Ali said to John, 'Just wait another six months, and then if you still want to leave, then leave. I've never asked anything of you before, but just hang in there. If we have to we will remortgage the house—just give it six more months'. John agreed.

It was while John was in the midst of these dark days that things began to heat up within the mobile communications industry. Just a few months into Ali's six-month deadline, Cable & Wireless Optus Communications was granted Australia's second general carrier license.

It represented a huge moment and led to a complete deregulation of the telecommunications industry. Alongside Telstra, Optus could now begin battling for a slice of the

$1 billion a year mobile phone market. Competition could finally be encouraged.

Although Optus was initially only permitted to enter the Australian market for national long distance and international telephone calls, it soon moved into other telecommunication services, including mobile phones. Significantly, Optus opened a shop across the road from John's Brunswick store, and for the first time Telstra was forced to think about the way it was doing business.

Optus had introduced a trial of commissions to its dealers of one to two per cent. This meant that dealers could now make money from the ongoing revenue generated from their customers, the logic being that dealers could then afford to reduce the handset costs and therefore attract more people to the network.

Telstra had never offered this type of incentive to its dealers, and had to follow suit in order to remain competitive. Its customers were tired of the telco's lack of customer service and had been leaving in droves. But Telstra needed to find dealers to sell on its behalf, and with Optus opening a shop over the road from John's, the telco saw Mobileworld as a way to create competition.

In what would represent a huge turning point in John's life, Telstra invited him to become a dealer. It offered him an incentive of $30 for every phone that he sold, and ironically, the moment occurred almost to the day that Ali instructed him to hold on for another six months. 'You should have seen the look on his face', Ayse recalls. 'Things were finally starting to fall into place.' Of course John accepted the offer, recognising that he could really start to drive the business forward with the backing of one of the giants of the industry. It was the beginning of his success.

It was also the beginning of another relationship—between John and his future wife, Patricia. At the time, Telstra needed to do something to lure back the customers who had left. To do so it went into a recruitment overdrive, hiring staff accustomed to working in aggressive markets. One of its new recruits was Patricia Sequenzia, an account dealer manager. She was a twenty-six-year-old University of Melbourne graduate, with a Bachelor of Arts degree majoring in psychology.

After knocking back an offer to study honours in psychology, Patricia accepted an offer from IBM following a university recruitment drive by some of the larger corporates. She spent seven years at the company selling mid-range systems as a corporate representative and loved it. Her products were always fifteen per cent more expensive than the competition and she relished operating in a fiercely competitive market. IBM was forward-thinking too, and provided her with great opportunities to travel and train overseas, including teaching new graduates in Hong Kong for several weeks at a time.

However, IBM was in major financial difficulty. Patricia's ability to move up through the ranks was hampered by the company's money problems, and she decided that she had had enough. Her sister Diana was already working at Telstra as a paging account manager and she knew the team in the mobile department, which was one floor up. Diana called Patricia and told her about a new position in the mobile department that she thought would be ideal for her.

Although it was not a new market Diana knew that Patricia was looking for a new challenge. Patricia applied for the job, was offered it and resigned from IBM straightaway. She had a proven track record in a highly competitive and mature industry and that was what Telstra needed to ensure the future of the business. Assuming that the telecommunication industry would go the way of the computer industry, Telstra was recruiting heavily from that field.

Patricia was offered the job in 1991 and began working solidly for her new company. Across town John was starting out, but making progress with his own business. He had already been appointed a dealer manager by Telstra.

In mid 1993 Patricia was handed a portfolio of about thirty mobile phone dealers, a considerably easier number than she was used to at IBM. But then she took a closer look at one of the dealers in her portfolio, John Ilhan at Mobileworld Communications. The rep noted while handing the file to her, 'Just babysit him. He's never going to make anything of himself'. Patricia assumed he was just another insignificant fly-by-night dealer. Her career was important to her, and it was vital that she ensured her dealers did well as a reflection of her own abilities.

As they began working together Patricia would regularly drive out to John's store in Brunswick. 'He was only about twenty-six', she recalls. 'He was very young in most respects and very quiet. I used to have to brief him before meetings with Telstra, and he was so shy. Before we went into meetings I'd say, "It's really important you have a presence about you. You need to make sure you're being heard. I've organised this meeting with senior managers but I can't be seen to do all the talking". Even through the meetings, I'd have to prompt him. It got to a point where that chip on his shoulder would come out. It was all about proving that he was something.'

It was clear from those early meetings that John had a different agenda to Patricia. She took her job very seriously and was already in a relationship. 'I'd come into the meeting with this structured format and say, "Okay. These are the topics we are going to discuss today" and he'd whisper, "Let's have a cup of coffee". He just had no boundaries. I had this clear boundary that it's a professional environment, so I would ignore him. I was seeing someone else at the time ... and it was so inappropriate. But he didn't care about that.'

'I had worked very hard to get to where I was—a good wage and respectable position—and here's this young floozy from Broady constantly distracting me while I have targets to achieve, some of which I was being paid on. My job was quite serious to me.

'This went on for some time, maybe two years. And then there came a point when I was meeting my sisters and their husbands at a restaurant in Carlton and John had been saying all day, "Let's just have a coffee". So I rang him and asked if he wanted to pop in and have coffee, and he came with a friend. We had pizza and that was the beginning of our relationship.'

Patricia, like John, knew that she had found her soul mate. 'He had a lot of energy, determination and more ambition than I've ever seen in anyone. I respected him in business too. Here's a bloke who's had no mentor and a very poor level of education. Yet he had such a good grasp of human nature. He understood people, he could read them, and he understood the tricks of the trade. I thought that in some respects he knew so much more than me, yet I'd had all the advantages, and he'd come from nothing and picked all this up along the way. Life had taught him. Maybe it was survival. You have to know how to talk your way out of things.'

'Three months after we started going out he took me to dinner—it was my thirtieth birthday. [We went to] a restaurant near Camberwell Junction. At one point I just said to him at the dinner table, "You're going to be my husband and you're going to be the father of my children". He was drinking a coffee and he spat it out across the table. He said, "How could you possibly know that?" I said, "I'm not in any hurry, I just know it's going to be you".'

Luckily for John his father asking him to hold onto the business for another six months was perhaps his most valuable piece of advice. And John, fuelled by pride and a deep desire not to fail, had ploughed on. 'I remember John saying that everyone gets a chance to be successful, they just don't do something with that chance', says Ali. 'Sometimes people see the risk as too great or others just miss seeing it as a chance. The difference was John knew when he opened the business it was the right thing to do, he just needed to work through those initial hardships.'

Chapter 6

Let's get crazy

1993–1996

It was the break John had been waiting for. With his new status as a Telstra reseller he now had to find a way to penetrate the market and he realised very quickly that price was the key. It seemed the best way to get noticed by Telstra was to sell a lot of phones and start slashing the cost of the expensive technology.

Most customers still thought of mobiles as yuppie toys— too expensive and only for businesspeople or the wealthy. They also still cost in excess of $5400 each. John believed if he could break through the barrier in the mind of the consumer and turn the mobile phone into an everyday necessity, he could really start turning his business around.

John's philosophy was that if he sold enough phones at a discount, Telstra would ask him to be a premier dealer. His logic was simple: why not slash the margins to encourage more people to buy phones? While Telstra was making high margins selling fewer phones, John reversed the tactic, offering more phones at a lower cost.

To reach his market he needed to advertise. John had decided that whatever spare money he had would be spent on advertising, based on the positive response he had received from placing small ads in the *Herald Sun* and the *Trading Post*. However, it was not until he teamed up with Sean Taylor, the then sales director at radio station Triple M, that John's Mobileworld Communications began to find its feet.

John had contacted the station to enquire about advertising during the breakfast program, and Sean saw the potential in John's fledgling business and decided to work with him to help grow it. Sean and John had agreed that they couldn't cut through the market by offering a price-discount platform alone. There was plenty of competition from other burgeoning mobile phone companies, and they both knew the business needed something extra to give it an edge.

One day in 1993 Sean received a call from one of John's competitors. 'John is crazy!' said one of Sean's clients, referring to John's advertised low prices. The comment clicked instantly and Sean thought about how he could use it. 'So I actually pitched the name "Crazy John's" to John, but not as a name, as a character in a commercial. He said no [concerned it would hinder rather than help the business] and we had a bit of a debate about it for a while. It was all about building the brand, though', Sean says. Eventually John relented. A mate of Sean's—John Hillier—drew up a design for the character for about $50, comprising a maniacal-looking man with unruly hair, bulging crossed eyes and lolling tongue, and the Crazy John's mascot was born.

The strategy was to try to capture the twenty-five to thirty-nine-year-old male demographic. John knew exactly what his demographic did—they went out to nightclubs and out for dinner and wanted to be able to keep in touch with friends they were planning to meet up with—and needed to create a way to attract this market. The premise was that Crazy John's had so many cheap deals it was 'crazy'. However, when a customer entered the store the experience was the exact opposite—while there were plenty of crazy deals, the staff were knowledgeable, friendly and efficient. It all helped develop the image of Crazy John's. The name of the business was initially changed to Crazy John's at Mobileworld Communications, before it was eventually shortened to Crazy John's. This process took about two years.

John thought it was a perfect fit, but Telstra hated it. The telco thought the name was silly, not conservative enough, and insisted that he change it. Telstra didn't feel that 'Crazy John's' portrayed a professional image, and said it smacked of discount and diminished quality.

John stuck to his guns. 'I just wanted something that was a bit more fun and appealing to the masses', he said. 'Why do people have this idea that to be good in business you have to be serious? I've never understood that and I disagree with it—I think people want to enjoy the retail experience. Just because they are making an important buying decision and possibly spending a lot of money, why can't they have a good time doing it?'

John likened his brand to Virgin. 'Can you imagine the amount of flack Richard Branson must have received when he called his company Virgin—especially in the UK. It would have been offensive to some people, yet look at the brand now. It's a global phenomenon.' However, Crazy John's was hardly Virgin. Unlike the major top-selling dealers who were Telstra's 'preferred suppliers', Crazy John's was in the bottom half of the playing field.

In 1994 Crazy John's began to get crazy. John put his price-slashing strategy into action and started to offer bargain-basement prices with designer-store service. He significantly reduced the cost of handsets—a move that was a first in the industry. It would be the first of many strategies to come.

By far his most successful and well-remembered campaign was offering phone deals for $1. One of his early employees and good friends, Ash Rady, remembers how popular the $1 gimmick was. 'It was a Motorola Flare phone. Telstra was struggling to move a particular type of handset, and they put forward an offer on a handset that brought the price down below the rebate and still left margin built into the handset. So John was effectively able to offer that phone on a plan—to give it away—and still make good gross profit from selling that product. It was the first time the industry [had seen] an offer that aggressive.

'We couldn't mention $1 as there was a rule effectively put in place to prevent us from offering that deal. The ads were already produced and many thousands of dollars were pumped into creating the content of the ad, but we couldn't verbally communicate the $1 deal. So John came up with the idea that we didn't have to verbally communicate it all, we'd just show a $1 coin rolling on the screen. The traffic still came in and we sold thousands of those units.

'It was really a milestone. No-one had ever offered a handset for $1. We're used to it today, but you've got to go back to that time when phones just a year or two prior were running into the thousands. To offer a phone for $1 was amazing at that time.'

To make Crazy John's customers feel welcome the shop resembled a lounge room. There were about ten desks and comfortable seats from which to complete the paperwork, and a staff member was always on hand to answer any questions. It was more like sitting in a friend's lounge room than waiting for service in a phone shop.

Back then the connection was not instantaneous the way it is now. There was no SIM card with a pre-allocated number; the phone was blank until it was connected. Customers would fill out all the paperwork in the shop and be given their handset. The sales clerk would then select a number from a sequential list supplied by Telstra and allocate that number to the phone. But until the paperwork had been approved and the number connected, the handset was technically 'empty'. This meant customers could actually go to another dealer and connect with it, so it was important to get approval as soon as possible.

The industry norm was to fill in the paperwork and fax it through to Telstra for approval, which could take up to ten days. But not at Crazy John's—staff would chase Telstra for the approval and connection. Then the sales clerk that made the initial sale would call the customer to welcome them to Crazy John's. Not only was this great customer service, but also it made shrewd business sense. Crazy John's ensured maximum connections in minimum time, and got to make the first phone call to the customer and use it as a customer service check to ensure the customer was totally happy with the purchase and knew how to operate the phone. In those days the staff would also program phone numbers into the phone for the customer and this combination of swift and considerate service made Crazy John's very popular.

One of Crazy John's longstanding employees, George Midas, started working for John in 1992 at the Brunswick store. George has been with Crazy John's ever since, working in a number of positions, including running the Mitcham store with John's sister Ayse, who joined the business in 1994. He is now the National Sales Manager for Business Solutions based at the South Melbourne head office. George remembers the early days and the importance placed on customer service—in particular, on product knowledge. 'The Brunswick store was stale and smelt of smoke, because back then we were allowed to smoke in the store, and you could smell coffee as there was a coffee shop next door', he says. 'Back then to activate a customer was a lengthy process, and you were spending at least an hour with a customer, minimum, so you'd buy them coffee and have a cigarette with them.'

George recalls that he was not allowed to speak to a single customer until he had read every manual for the phones Crazy John's sold. He had to know the programming of every phone by heart to be able to answer any questions the customer might have had. 'We had a room right at the back, which was like the finance room. John gave me a box of manuals, and said to me, "George, you're going to learn every single phone back to front". Now, I don't know if he initiated every staff member like that, but he made me read all these manuals. Back then, there were no SIM cards so you had to program the phone number into the phone, including all of the Australian codes, so there were about five different things that related to our network that we had to program into the phone, otherwise it wouldn't work. I had to learn features and technical specifications too. About two weeks later he allowed me to sell on the floor', he says.

John knew that having good staff made all the difference. He had learnt this from his experience at Strathfield, which translated into more sales and revenue. Ultimately, his wish was for his customers to feel welcomed and listened to. He knew that they would probably be feeling apprehensive about the choices available, the jargon in the contract and what the best product for them was, but John ensured they were reassured and were saving money in the long run. The customers were thrilled because they were getting access to a product that they couldn't previously afford, and John was happy because his stores were filling up. His brand was gaining awareness, too, plus he was actually making some revenue.

'If people are honest with customers and say thank you and show the customer a bit of respect, they will stay', argued John. 'If I was a steam cleaner and I steam cleaned your home and sent a red rose with the invoice, would you stay with me? Would you tell half-a-dozen people? Of course you would, and it would [have cost me] next to nothing.'

By the start of 1993 John had employed a handful of staff. To keep costs down, he hired staff using the Commonwealth Employment Service (CES), where the government offered incentives to employers to hire people who had been unemployed for certain periods of time, such as paying half their wage. At that stage the store hierarchy consisted of John at the helm and his staff beneath him. As he expanded he would appoint a manager for each store, but he was always at the top making the crucial decisions.

At the same time, while customers were still leaving Telstra in droves, another event caused huge upheaval to the telecommunications industry. Following the recommendation of the industry regulator Austel, a third carrier was granted a license. This time it was UK-based Vodafone, which paid $140 million to enter the telecommunications industry. With $1 billion earmarked for infrastructure development, Vodafone was a powerful force and stores started springing up nationally as the new carrier staked its claim in the lucrative market. Vodafone's weight as the third carrier was certainly felt within the industry, which was continuing to grow like few others before it.

As the business began to pick up John was able to buy stock on credit, but his parents continued to pour their savings into the business. By this stage John had sold the land that Ali and Nezaket had bought him, and Gerald had done the same and given the cash to John. But everything at Crazy John's was still very basic. All of John's meetings were conducted two doors down at Jack's Milk Bar, while everything from light fittings to electrical power boards were bought as cheaply as possible to help with the business. 'In the end all we had left was the family house, but we were the happiest family with absolutely no regrets other than wishing there was more we could do', says Ayse. John's parents tried to do everything they could to help John's business grow, including withdrawing money they had invested in Turkey and putting it into the business, and giving him money that they had inherited from their parents.

The guy who had been a waste of time was suddenly making a difference to Telstra's bottom line, and simply by thinking of new ways to market his products he was able to massively grow his company in a short period of time. Not only was his shop busy, which meant more revenue, but his increasing stock turnover allowed him to negotiate even better deals with manufacturers.

John soon graduated to selling new accessories. He was also the first with 'cash back' and 'two-for-one' offers, plus Crazy John's became known as the Accessories King. John was able to secure accessories with a supposed high value for customers, which were bundled in the most attractive way before being marketed through press advertising.

In Sydney Road, Brunswick, competition between the new Optus store, Crazy John's and Strathfield Car Radio was thriving. Customers now had greater choice, more flexibility and were being delivered a higher level of service by the competing companies.

At one point an accessories war broke out between Crazy John's and Strathfield Car Radio as both tried to outdo each other in giving away the most accessories. Starting at three, Strathfield upped the offer to four, John came back with five, and so it went on. John won at thirteen. George Midas remembers it all well. 'The other dealers hated us. And they knew the volume of business we were doing because Telstra would publish league table ratings. We were connecting more people in a month in Victoria than other companies were connecting nationally.'

John's advertising relationship with Sean Taylor and Triple M was also helping him build his name. Meetings would always be held at nearby Jack's Milk Bar. 'My first impressions were that he was one of many in what was an emerging market—mobile phones', Sean recalls. 'My job was to go through our client list and grow people's businesses, and as much as it was a small store, it was backed by Telstra and had some credibility. So we tried lots of different things to get some sort of cut through into his target male demographic.'

Of the many different stunts, John and Sean's biggest brand-building success was Triple M's 'live reads' campaign. Each morning, a sixty-second Crazy John's commercial was presented to consumers by the Richard Stubbs Breakfast Show, which also included Tim Smith and Bridget Duclos. It was part of a six-month advertising strategy. It was basically a commercial read live-to-air, scripted, and featuring a Crazy John's story that had been dreamed up by scriptwriters. The idea was that consumers would tune in and listen to the live read every morning.

'They were hilarious and some of the stunts we created were fantastic. They were always newsworthy and written within forty-eight hours of going to air. When Crazy John's started getting some traction, there was a whole Crazy family:

Crazy John's wife, Crazy John's children, even Crazy George [Midas] was down there at the store. This thing basically took off', says Sean.

It was during the live-reads phase that John would cross paths with another famous Broady boy, Eddie McGuire, former Channel Nine boss and president of the AFL's Collingwood Football Club. 'I first met John in 1992 when I was working on the Richard Stubbs Breakfast Show on Triple M with Tim Smith and Bridget Duclos, and we were told we had to do these mobile phone adverts for a company called Crazy John's. I thought to myself, what a stupid name, but it stuck in my mind', Eddie recalls.

'We had to read these ads over the air and we actually had to write the scripts and everything, and we were mucking around trying to create something funny. The amazing thing was that John was really happy with the ads.

'We had to go out to the Brunswick store as part of the deal, so I went out there with Bridget and Tim, and that's when we met John. Over coffee I realised the Broadmeadows connection and we got talking and I suddenly realised I liked the guy. That's when he convinced me to buy my first mobile phone—and it was a brick. So I went from not wanting to go out to Brunswick to see the store to buying a phone—that was John for you. And I've stayed with Crazy John's ever since.

'Actually buying those radio ads really was a big deal and it showed how much courage John had, because the Richard Stubbs Breakfast Show was the top-rating radio show at the time and on-air advertising wasn't cheap, yet he paid for an ad campaign when he only had one store. It showed he wasn't afraid to be bold.

'[John and I] did all our deals on a handshake. We had a good gut instinct that we would look after each other. I could see what was in a deal for him and vice versa. I mean, if we needed \$10 000 to bring out an artist to perform on *The Footy Show*, I'd ring up John and he'd say yes straightaway, and I'd say we'd look after him with plenty of mentions on the show and we knew we'd both win out.

'When I became president of Collingwood and we needed funds to rebuild the club, I went to see John. I knew he was a Richmond supporter and he loved soccer, but John saw the vision of what we were trying to do and he came on board right away. He was one of our first supporters and helped save the club and I'll never forget that.'

There were many other strange campaigns over the years. One was the midnight-to-morning sale. Triple M would promote the sale as something a little different and presenters would roll up in the customised four-wheel drives, park outside the store and deliver the show live on-site, as part of an outside broadcast. The party atmosphere attracted customers who would drop in after a night out on the town and end up buying a phone. There was even a sausage sizzle on offer and people would line up for 100 metres to get into the store in the middle of the night.

John's pet campaign, however, was his car park sales. Friend and former employee Ash Rady recalls, 'He'd get all the old stock that we had in the company, take it to the Brunswick store's car park and advertise a weekend car park sale. He'd get hundreds and hundreds of people. All the dead stock that we had in the company would just fly out the door. Some of it discounted, some of it not discounted.

'We had security and [the sale] drew a crowd. The TV advertising that John put together before was the first genuine clearance sale advertisements with the emphasis and the hype that you see in today's commercials. John really did start that form of marketing—ads promoting sales at the exhibition buildings and clearance sales', he says.

Ash had joined the business in 1996, but had known John since they were teenagers. Their friendship and future business relationship almost never happened because their first meeting nearly came to blows. Ash was nineteen, John one or two years older. 'It was at Broadmeadows shopping centre— I was in my car and John was in his car with his parents. John and I didn't know each other. He was driving his car and he screeched around the corner and nearly wiped my car off. John completely cut me off and we got into a fairly heated argument', Ash recalls.

Unbeknown to John, Ash had formed a friendship with John's brother Gerald a few months before, and had driven to the shopping centre as he had done on a number of previous occasions to catch up with his new mate for a coffee. 'After I'd gone into the shopping centre and met up with Gerald, I saw John walking down towards us and I thought, "Okay, this guy wants to have a bit of an argument". He came up and said a few words and I can't remember the words that he used but he called me a smart arse or something to that effect. Anyway we got into another argument there in the shopping centre and then Gerald introduced us. He introduced John as his brother and we started laughing about it afterwards, but that's how John and I met and we became good friends from that point on.'

In the early 2000s Ash travelled to Queensland to meet with a company called Electronics Boutique and set up a deal where customers were given an Xbox if they signed up for a particular handset. Electronics Boutique was able to sell Crazy John's its product at cost price, as its money was made through the software not the hardware. Customers simply signed up for the handset, redeemed the voucher they would be issued with at an Electronics Boutique store, and the Xbox was theirs. The campaign was a huge success.

John's unorthodox approach and discounting strategy earned him a reputation for being a cowboy, but in reality it was simply aggressive marketing. He always did the right thing by giving the customer the best deal and, ultimately, the better he performed, the better Telstra's coffers were lined. It was a win–win situation.

'People get boxed in by what's been done before, especially within industries, so they may look around within their industry to see what's been done', said John. 'I say go bigger. Have a look at all industries and other countries and cultures to see if there are things you like that are clever, and cross-pollinate them from one industry to another. What can be humdrum in one field can be cutting edge in another, so keep an open mind.'

Ash maintains that John was exceptionally clever to recognise the potential in the telecommunications industry. 'Obviously Telstra was looking for [stores] they could help grow and build, and John had the ability to sell ice to Eskimos. There were many other players in the market at the time, but only a very small number of them were able to capitalise on that shift in the market. John saw the opportunity and had the vision to understand that things were changing, and he positioned himself beautifully to capture that growth.

'[Crazy John's] was growing at a rate that certainly a company like Telstra would have taken notice of, and as it was looking for dealers to partner with I'm sure John's business was on the radar. From that point on John took the opportunity and obviously was able to ride that wave—that wave of growth as a result of competition entering the market. Optus was certainly a threat to Telstra and John saw the time to grow was then.'

In 1994 Telstra began to offer an incentive to dealers to open up new shops close to its competitors. The promise was that the giant business would provide funds if the store operators could get the new stores up and running.

When the offer was made to John, he didn't hesitate for a second. Opening any new store involved risk, but for John that was but a blip when he looked at the bigger picture. He could potentially secure tens of thousands of dollars from Telstra to expand his operations.

He didn't care about forecasting future sales to determine whether he would break even, about staffing issues or the extra work, or ponder how he was going to fit out the new stores and refurbish them appropriately, he simply focused on the positives. And although the extra cash was largely insufficient to cover all the costs involved in setting up new stores, it would still provide a window of opportunity he wouldn't otherwise have. So while others dithered and considered and procrastinated and number crunched, John just said yes.

In 1994 he opened his second store in Campbellfield, followed by South Melbourne, Mitcham and Dandenong. As John began to open new stores, Triple M was right there with him. The radio station continued its popular outside broadcasts, with staff on hand with giveaways. There was a great atmosphere with people queuing up outside the store to buy phones. The Dandenong store opening, in particular, was a great event. By this stage John had begun exploring a strategy of opening clusters of phone stores in the same area.

'Some of those early broadcasts were incredible, because the thing was that people didn't actually need mobile phones. At 1.00 am, there'd be 200 people queuing around the corner to buy a phone. It was absolutely unbelievable', recalls Sean.

'The whole marketplace was what really drove the need for a mobile phone. The idea was that you needed a phone to be cool, and John was doing things like reconditioning old phones and allowing people to get into the market cheaply. For him it was all about acquisition, and that's what he did very well. He wasn't greedy with his margins and added value to the package, which was all the bonus components. He started that here in Australia.'

Crazy John's was the first privately owned dealership in Australia to have its own 'churn centre'. The centre operated in a similar way to a telemarketing business, although the numbers called were not random, they were actually Optus customers that Telstra tried to lure back with incentives. Telstra realised it was cheaper to retain customers than recruit them, and offered John money for every customer he brought back to Telstra. Once again it channelled a request through the account managers that they would jump on board financially if a dealer set up the churn centre. Of course, John jumped in. He found some low-rent office space above a shop and hired thirty telemarketers. The business became quite profitable and his team converted about fifty customers a day. The exercise was a success and strengthened his bond with Telstra.

Part of John's success lay in trying to create business 'firsts'. For example, it was John who introduced digital phones to the Australian marketplace.

In 1994 John hired his sister Ayse to help him in the business, and she remained at Crazy John's for the rest of John's career there. Ayse left her job to join her brother and, as well as helping with the finances, would later run the Mitcham store with George Midas. When she joined the business there were three Crazy John's stores. She managed the Brunswick store during a time when there was thirteen staff.

At the start of that year mobile phone connections broke the magic million, and despite reports of potential health risks from mobile phones being reported in the media, the industry showed no signs of slowing down. Australians had taken to mobile phones with a fervour in much the same way that they would eventually take to plasma televisions and the latest DVD players.

Each salesperson had an index card that stayed alphabetically in a card file box. Every time a salesperson took a product out of stock to show a customer, he or she would write down what product they took. At the end of the day the invoices from the sales were married up against the cards to indicate which stock items had been sold. If there wasn't an invoice for an item, it would be marked off the card again and put back into stock. With customers queuing out the door the system didn't always run according to plan.

At night each store would tally everything up and drive the cash and invoices to Ayse in Brunswick. 'Then I'd take it all home and go through all the paperwork for all the stores and make sure everything tallied and the money matched the invoices', recalls Ayse. 'Next morning I'd go to the bank and deposit it. The teller would be horrified at the amount of cash I used to carry around—it was crazy.'

Ayse also remembers another of John's 'projects'—one that grew so large and so quickly, and no-one had any idea just how successful it would become. John and Gerald began a mobile phone service and repair centre, with the intention of servicing Crazy John's customers as an addition to after-sales service. It was called ADM Services, and it was the only centre to have repair agreements for all manufacturers at the time. It would grow to become the largest privately owned service and repair centre in the southern hemisphere.

The centre was set up like a laboratory with anti-static flooring and bench tops and high-tech security. It received worldwide interest because of its unique selling point—repair agreements with all manufacturers—and many people would visit from all over the world to see how it operated.

Ayse recalls, 'We were growing both businesses simultaneously. But then a Singaporean company made John an offer and he sold it. This centre first opened a few months after the South Melbourne store opened in the same building as Crazy John's head office. It grew at such a rate it later relocated to Spencer Street, West Melbourne. The new owners renamed it Accord Customer Care and it is still in operation at the same location.'

John sold the business with just one condition — the existing staff had to be retained for a minimum of twelve months. The condition was upheld and the new owner rang John not long after to tell him how pleased he was with the staff. Some of them are still with Accord Customer Care today.

With John it was all or nothing. There was no in between, but simply a man of extremes. He expected the same of his staff, and his philosophy was that his business was his family. He found the right balance between having high expectations and enforcing them with genuine care and affection, especially for those who had been with him the longest.

John was the first to admit, 'I'm not good with detail. If you want to present something to me, make sure you can tell me about it in five minutes and keep reports down to one page wherever possible. I have the attention span of a gnat. But I know people, I know what they want before they do sometimes, and if you can talk to people and communicate your idea with passion, you can do anything. The way I keep across the detail of the business is by having the right team around me and asking people how they feel.'

As his business began to expand, some unsavoury aspects of the industry reared their head and plenty of people wanted to see him undone. As John told it, 'The business was really rough and ready in the early days. It was unregulated and had attracted some interesting people. I had people coming into the shop with sacks full of mobile phones, which were obviously stolen. I said no [to buying the stolen phones], and they would threaten me and push me against the wall. Looking back they were scary times but I didn't know any different, I'd grown up in rough areas my whole life. I thought life was a battle zone so it didn't faze me.'

Despite the fact that the business was becoming more successful, John's industry problems persisted. When he opened the Campbellfield store in 1994 a couple of men paid him a visit in his Brunswick store and made it pretty clear they were not very happy about the new store. John said they told him, 'We see you've opened a shop in Campbellfield. We'll give you two weeks to close it down'.

The intimidation continued. Notes were shoved under the windscreen of his car threatening to 'get him' if he didn't shut up shop. Staff were followed home from the store and threatened. John ensured that his female staff all carried mobile phones and that they were fully charged at all times without exception. Not only was this a safety measure, but also it allowed him to be in contact with his staff. In another incident someone took to the store with an axe. Staff members, including John, would finish up for the day only to find their tyres slashed. John reported these incidences to the police, but it was never proven who was responsible.

John recalled, 'The nicest people were not running phone retail businesses. The industry wasn't mature and there was an element of thuggery that got rid of some of the smaller competitors. I remember one dealer who sold accessories being visited by guys with guns in their briefcases … he got out [of the telecommunications industry] as it was just too dangerous.

People were being threatened and bullied, and not just them but their families too.'

John's family continued their support during this time. In particular, his brother Gerald offered his own kind of support. Gerald was into fitness and kickboxing, and ran with a different crowd. Although he wasn't involved in anything illegal, he was a well-built man and had a few connections. When the heavies who were threatening John realised who his brother was, they backed off.

Ultimately, Crazy John's was John's family and he expected everyone in the business to be as passionate about it as he was. There was no distinction between work and life for John. Every day was a Crazy John's day, and that meant Saturdays and Sundays, too. He made sure that he had a team around him that complemented his weaknesses.

Ash recalls John's ability to always think of the person first. 'He understood that his staff's lives were linked to their work and personal lives. If he was able to align their personal goals with that of the business, he'd get the most out of his employees, and he did that very well—he did that beautifully. I know he had a genuine regard for individuals and the challenges they had in life. Without work they couldn't achieve their personal goals and vice versa.'

In return John did not base success and reward solely upon results, rather it was based on attitude, effort and loyalty. The management structure was deliberately flat so that John and his senior team could stay close to the business, and this also kept it as transparent as possible.

He would always answer his own mobile phone for staff or clients. He said: 'I still answer my phone and if I miss the call I always call back. It's how you build relationships by showing respect, and that's done through the small things like returning phone calls today, not tomorrow or next week. I'll always do that regardless of the size of the business.'

John would bend over backwards for those who had done the same for him. He devised regular incentive schemes, bonus schemes that were excessive by industry standards, and held a yearly Crazy John's overseas company conference. A panel of department heads and managers would nominate who they thought should be recognised and send them on an all-expenses-paid overseas trip for a few weeks. He awarded all staff, from the courier to his senior staff, with profit share every year, and rather than replacing staff who may not have had skills in a particular area, he would retrain them or relocate them to another more suitable area. Loyalty bonuses were also awarded to long-time staff, who were given extra money as part of their package. Some staff members even received nannies to assist them if they had just had a baby and were struggling.

On one occasion he sent a number of staff members to Turkey following a series of earthquakes in late 1999. The trips were not part of an incentive scheme or bonus; John's immediate reaction was to pay for their flight so they could go back and support their families.

John relied on his gut instinct when it came to his employees and liked to give 'wild cards' a go, according to George Midas. 'He was really good at selecting people with good values, maybe not with the best education or the best upbringing. He saw the potential and nine times out of ten he was spot on.' The fact that a handful of his first employees were recruited from the Commonwealth Employment Service and that some of those, including George, still work at Crazy John's is testament to his good instincts.

George's employment at Crazy John's started a little rockily, when he found himself wondering when and if he was going to be paid after a month of accruing parking tickets and finding it hard to make ends meet. He gathered the courage and tentatively asked John when he thought he might be paid. 'John laughed at me and I think he felt bad because it wasn't that he didn't want to pay me. In hindsight I think he was probably either trying to teach me a lesson or trying to find out what sort of person I was by testing how long I could work without confronting him. John always said good things come to people who don't ask, so I think it was a test, and I passed it.'

Over the years John did little things such as pay George's phone bill or reward him with cash bonuses. He even loaned him his Porsche so George could take his wife away. But there was one occasion in 2003 that particularly stood out. 'I wanted my children to meet their only remaining grandmother and see where my father was brought up in Greece', George recalls. 'I approached John's PA, Natasha, and said, "Just let John know that I'm planning a trip", because anything over four weeks long had to be approved by John.

'My wife started booking flights and accommodation and I decided to take a month of my long-service leave. That day I got a call from Natasha saying, "John wants to see you". I thought there was something wrong and I was really paranoid. But I've gone to see him and he said, "I hear you want to go to Greece". I said, "Yeah, I do", and I thought that he was going to knock back my holiday. So I said, "John, before you say anything these are the reasons", and he said, "No, no, I'm not questioning why, because I can appreciate why you want to go to Greece". Then he started asking me when I was going and for how long and that sort of thing. He then calls in his PA and said, "Natasha, George is going to Greece. I want you to book his flights first class, I want you to organise all the accommodation, and by the way organise some spending money for him".

'I was beside myself, I didn't know what to say—I was really speechless. I did not expect that. I know he is very, very generous but I didn't expect that. All in all, that trip—just air flights and accommodation—was about twenty-five or thirty grand, so it was about a fifty grand holiday.'

In return Crazy John's staff were loyal, hardworking and trustworthy. In 1996 when the business was suffering heavily and the creditors were beating at the door and threatening to remove office furniture and computer equipment, staff inside locked the doors. Some staff accepted a huge pay cut during this time and were rewarded generously when the business picked up again with some of the best packages in the industry. There were staff members willing to drive interstate overnight to save the cost of couriers, as well as staff who worked through the night to do stocktakes.

That is not to say that John was not a hard taskmaster. As quick as he was to praise, he was also quick to give negative feedback, and this was the Crazy John's environment. Staff knew exactly where they stood with him and John was always very quick to deal with issues.

Ash remembers, 'John had to get his way—without question he had to get his way. But he'd do it in a way where he wouldn't yell or shout unless it got to a point where he had to repeat himself several times. John hated repeating himself. He wanted to say something once and he wanted people to follow that instruction, which is fair enough and how it should be. He was certainly a general in his handling of his business, and he saw business in a similar way to that of a hierarchy. He was the general, and the general had a shared direction and the soldiers had to basically fulfil that. But he'd make people feel part of the process. It wasn't a dictatorship style of management. Everyone did what they had to do because they really did care about John and they did care about the business and they wanted the business to succeed. He was able to bring out the best in people.'

Interestingly, John never touched a laptop or sent an email. He simply spouted out whatever was in his head and it was up to the people around him to act. He always had a personal assistant who he relied on to send emails and manage his diary. But he never said no to meeting anyone and would always find space in his diary to see people, no matter what the request. One of his longest-serving personal assistants was Natasha, who he hired on the spot after she had waited on him at a restaurant in Mt Buller. It was just another example of the way his mind worked—seeing potential and acting spontaneously. He was always switched on.

John was particularly difficult during the Muslim holy month of Ramadan, when he would fast for thirty days. This meant no food or drink during daylight hours. John, who had been a heavy smoker, would not smoke during this period either. Staff learnt to be particularly wary of him around this time. The fact that Ramadan occurred when he found out that a number of his staff had been pocketing money illegally meant his reaction was all the more harsh. The offences had been building for some time, and it was unfortunate that Ramadan was in full swing, as he fired all twenty-three members of staff involved. However, John ended up apologising to most of those employees and hiring them back on a higher salary as compensation. In subsequent years, he would take the month off and stay at home.

John was the first to admit he had a terrible temper and could often get personal in disputes. 'I'd rather be nice to people all the time but it comes with the job. I have friends and family working at Crazy John's and sometimes I can be a nightmare. I know I hurt people and that's the downside of business. I could say my staff love me and I'm a really good bloke, but it's not true. I'm not always nice ... I'm not Mother Teresa.'

His unique philosophies worked, though. Crazy John's was right up there with its competitors and John's stores were really starting to turn around. The Brunswick store alone was making 800 to 1000 connections a month, compared with the 100 to 150 connections per store today. It seemed the mobile phone industry was recession-proof, with 660 000 people carrying a mobile phone at that time. Australians were the world's fourth most extensive users per head of population. John had easily made his first few million. However, it was not all smooth sailing, as Crazy John's would soon discover.

Chapter 7

Growing pains and growing large

1996–1998

Every fast-growing business hits a speed bump, but for John and the team at Crazy John's 1996 was a year that almost saw the demise of this emerging company. It was a year in which Crazy John's hit a cash-flow problem—and it was sizeable. The company owed about $4 million to suppliers and was owed about $1 million by Telstra (the telco had been delaying paying a significant commission instalment).

At the time, Crazy John's had a number of stores and had made its first foray into Queensland, opening three stores. The company had moved into Queensland with a strategy to later extend its network into Sydney, but had to wait three years to do so. The mobile phone market was growing quickly, and John was acutely aware that his business model worked—he was just trying to roll it out as fast as possible.

One of the stores he opened in Queensland was at Mermaid Beach on the Gold Coast. Several months later Ron Bakir opened a competing store two doors down from Crazy John's and called his store Crazy Ron's. John was not happy and expressed opposition to the name, but chose not to pursue the matter at that time.

John was dealing with the cash flow issue with his accountant and confidant Nick Mitsios, but it was decided that he needed more help. That was when an important figure entered John's life—Brendan Fleiter, the man who would eventually become John's right-hand man and Chief Executive of Crazy John's.

Brendan was a lawyer who specialised in insolvency. He was called to a meeting at Nick Mitsios's accounting firm in mid 1996. 'I went down to Nick's office in East Melbourne and met a fairly young John Ilhan and another guy called Mark Djemal who was then in the business, and they told me they had some problems', Brendan recalls. 'They told me there was money being withheld by Telstra over commissions, that several million dollars was owed to creditors, and that John was thinking about putting the company into administration.'

Crazy John's income was based around trailing comm-issions. When the company connects someone up to a mobile phone plan, the active connections create revenue for the company through its receipt of an ongoing 'trailer' commission. This commission is calculated as a percentage of the cost of any call made by the customer. The amount of the commission paid to any mobile phone dealer depends on a number of factors, but Crazy John's is understood to have had one of the more lucrative deals with Telstra, receiving in excess of ten per cent of the customer's total monthly bill.

Trailing commissions can be a profitable business—even in 1996 when the mobile phone market was only just getting started. Back then hundreds of millions of dollars were being spent each year on mobile phones in Australia. Today that figure is about $15 billion.

John knew the business model was not broken—and would become more lucrative as the mobile phone business grew—it was just that he had over-committed. For that reason he wasn't going to roll over without a fight. 'John told me firmly he wanted help to try to keep the business going. I remember the first day I met him. We got on very well and we went through the usual process of going through the details and appointing the administrator. My role at that time was to sort out what was a bit of a financial mess', says Brendan.

While John was dealing with the challenges of growing a business too quickly, he experienced something that would ultimately affect the way he lived the rest of his life. On 25 October 1996 John's brother Gerald was found dead in his apartment. The police report stated the cause of death was suicide, but the autopsy identified that Gerald had suffered a heart attack. He was only thirty-three years old and his death shook the family to the core. The Ilhans were never completely satisfied with the investigations into his death and they felt there were too many unanswered questions surrounding Gerald's passing. The event would act as an ominous warning for John's own future.

John was overcome with grief. By comparison his business problems suddenly didn't seem so important. What followed were John's darkest days. He went into a downward spiral of doubt and depression that lasted several months. 'I was at rock bottom. I was questioning everything, including God, and I just didn't care about the business at all. I think I was depressed', John said of the time.

During this time John also had trouble sleeping. On occasions he reported feeling an intense pressure on his chest as though someone was pushing down on him. He called his father about it one night, who reassured him that he had heard of this type of reaction after a sudden loss and that it was often a sign that the person should explore their spirituality.

A few weeks later John was at home watching television, trying to find something to take his mind off the grief and anger he felt. Flicking through the channels he caught sight of his reflection in the window opposite. It was an image of him on his knees praying. 'I know that some people will think I'm mad, but it was as clear as day, so vivid that I lent forward and tried to grab it. I was shocked and a bit freaked out', he said.

He sat staring at the reflection until it vanished. The strange experience moved him enough to start reading the Koran again and re-familiarise himself with the Bible. Although John was a Muslim he was not practising, but the vision inspired him to seek some answers. He began to pray again and returned to the mosque regularly rather than just on special occasions.

Reading these religious and spiritual texts lifted his spirit as he gained a greater understanding for what was happening in his life. He knew that he could not go on forever mourning Gerald. 'As crazy as it sounds when I tell it, and I'm sure it will sound even crazier when it's written in black and white, I know what I saw and it changed my life', said John. 'I surrendered my life to God in that moment and I've never looked back. All I can do now is my very best, do the right thing and it will work out. If it doesn't it wasn't God's plan.'

John believed in Judgement Day—he believed that there would come a time when he would be assessed to see if the good he had done during his life outweighed the bad. He said, 'This belief keeps me in my little box and gives me security. I like that boundary of fear because it keeps things simple. I think being a good person is the most important thing. People are more important than things. I value family far more than money, and that has allowed me to take risks in business that I may not otherwise have taken. If I'm not attached to money and it doesn't define me as a person, then I'm not that scared to lose it. Sure I'd rather keep it, but it's not who I am.'

While John was dealing with the trauma of losing his brother and the stress of saving his company, there was a positive and joyful event to occur that year—John and Patricia's wedding. Before Gerald died they had planned the union for January 1997, but were now worried about the timing. 'We were all devastated and it just didn't seem right to have a wedding so soon after the death', Patricia recalls. 'I was sure that we wouldn't get married for at least six months, but it had the opposite effect on John. It made him realise just how precious life is, and he didn't want to wait any longer before we got married and started a family.'

Arriving at this point had not been an easy road for John and Patricia. John was running a successful business, but the three years prior to their wedding had been incredibly difficult for both of them. According to Patricia, this period was the making of their relationship.

When they started dating Patricia had already bought her first house in Surrey Hills, a suburb in Melbourne's inner east, while John was still living with his parents. He was twenty-eight and Patricia was six months older. John had a lot on his plate in terms of the business and he was also heavily involved with soccer, training three nights a week and playing on the weekend. 'The classic argument was that between his business, playing soccer, and me, I ended up being the third', recalls Patricia. 'Looking back, those first few years were very turbulent times. John trying to manage the business, as well as the first serious relationship he'd had. I wanted a mature relationship and that was really stretching him. All he wanted to do was play soccer, and then I come along and say we're going to have a life together. It was all too much. There were many arguments when he'd turn his back and walk out the door to play soccer.'

There were further issues relating to Patricia's Catholic upbringing and John's Muslim background. As such, they often kept to themselves, with John attempting to shield Patricia from any potentially difficult family situations. They broke up twice during the early stage of the relationship, rendering Patricia unable to work for a period due to stress. 'It took three years for him to mature enough to make the commitment', Patricia says, but he finally got down on one knee and proposed.

Ali and Nezaket had realised that by this stage the pair were practically living together and they were ready for a deeper commitment. Patricia and John were living between Patricia's Surrey Hills house and a property John had bought in the blue-chip suburb of Brighton, on North Road, and Ali gave them his blessing to marry. Just a few days later, on 23 November 1996, Patricia and John were married in a whirlwind wedding. It was four weeks after Gerald had passed away.

The night before the wedding John had a chat to Patricia. 'I remember that night because he told me he had some money in the bank—a lot of money in the bank', says Patricia. 'I was shocked because he had never exhibited signs of it. The first time he came to my place he came empty-handed—I couldn't believe it. He says he brought himself and that should have been enough, but I was mortified!'

The money was actually millions and millions. Patricia was perfectly happy living in John's house in North Road, having a new BMW to drive and the opportunity to send their children to private school. News of a seven-figure amount meant they would enjoy a privileged life indeed, despite the fact that Patricia was already independent and expecting to work for the rest of her life. It was certainly a step up from John first turning up at her house empty-handed in his rusty old Toyota Celica.

John's family knew about the money, but it was never a big deal. His mother had taken the first $50 he ever made, from the second-hand pager, and put it in a separate bank account for him. She used to say that she would do this until there was $10 000 so that he would have a deposit for a house and whatever he did with anything else he made was up to him. Once the business really started to take off in 1993 and 1994 that figure went up to $20 000. The plan then changed so that she would keep $50 000 for him, then $100 000 until finally there was over a million dollars in the bank account.

It was not a big fairytale wedding; it was a traditional Islamic ceremony at the Ilhans' house. John's father organised a priest for a private service and the plans were set for a wedding only a few days after their engagement was announced. 'It was a typical Muslim wedding where the vows that you would normally make in a church are made at home and witnessed by all your family and friends. I just had my parents and my sisters and their husbands, and John had his sister and his parents there. John's mum did everything. She made all this beautiful food, she bought a beautiful white tablecloth and made a cake, too', recalls Patricia.

'I wasn't in a wedding dress; I was in a really nice suit, like we were going to Sunday mass. The Hoca [priest] came over and we sat in the lounge room, and every word was said in Turkish and Ayse translated everything for the benefit of my family. The condition of the marriage was that I had to convert to Islam. I had to say the five pillars of Islam with everybody witnessing them, and it was actually quite beautiful, it was like poetry.

'Then John's dad blessed the rings. They were on a heart-shaped cushion and they were joined by a red ribbon. His father said a prayer and he cut the ribbon and John put my ring on me and I put his ring on him. John's dad said to me that day, "The greatest blessing for our family was that you came to meet John and you came to us and we've waited all our lives for someone like you", and I'd only met him once before.'

A month later Patricia and John invited thirty people to a celebratory wedding dinner at a private room at Maxim's, the former restaurant in South Yarra. Patricia wore a white Grecian dress for the occassion, and they organised a photographer to take photos earlier in the day around Melbourne.

After they were married John and Patricia were both accepted and welcomed into each side of the family. John decided to give up soccer in an effort to commit seriously to his family. Their marriage also paved the way for others in the Turkish community, as Patricia explains. 'In John's world, a Muslim man or a Turkish man had never married an Australian or a non-Turkish woman and it had been a great success. So he walked on new ground by marrying me. After we were married we had so many young Turkish boys come up to us and say, "Thank you so much for making it work because you've allowed us the opportunity to mix with women outside our community".'

Another friendship blossomed around this time — John's relationship with Gerald's friend Seb Pir. Two weeks before Gerald died Seb had spent hours talking to him at the Broadmeadows Mosque, where they were both attending the Friday service. Seb and Gerald sat for so long that they found themselves completely alone after everybody had left, and the conversation affected Seb deeply. Seb did not see Gerald again, as he passed away just two weeks later. 'I lost my sister a long time ago, and I understood. His life was finished, but my life goes on', Seb says.

As a result, Seb became closer to the Ilhans and visited them constantly for a few weeks. At one stage, Nezaket asked, 'Who's this young man coming around and giving us so much support?' To which Ayse replied, 'He's been coming around every night and he was close to Gerald'. From that point on Seb was accepted into their family.

When the Pirs found out that John had married, Seb decided it was time for the two couples to get together, as his wife Sam and Patricia had never met. 'They came to our house for a barbeque', recalls Seb. 'They drove all the way from Brighton to Meadow Heights. When John walked in, and he had that beautiful smile on his face, I pulled him aside and said to him, "John, I'd like to say something to you. You know all those years at soccer? I actually thought you were stuck up, but you're not. You were just very quiet. I always used to ask your brother why you don't talk. But it's better you hear it from me than somebody else". John said, "Me? Of all people! Stuck up? I'm none of those things!" "No, I believe you", I said.' The families developed a strong bond over the years. Seb shares his star sign with John, as Sam does with Patricia. The couple has three boys and one girl—Ferah, Azim, Taner and Mikail—the opposite of John and Patricia.

During 1997 John and Patricia reached another milestone. Their first child, Yasmin, was born in October. The difficulties of the previous year had taken their toll on John, especially with the company in administration, but he never brought work home, so Patricia never knew how bad the business was.

Once Yasmin was born she was busy being a new mother and readily admits, 'I had no idea it was as bad as it was. Yasmin wasn't sleeping and I don't even remember the first six months. She would sleep for five minutes each hour and I was going insane from sleep deprivation, so to be honest even if he'd told me, I was exhausted and overwhelmed at being a new mother [so I wouldn't have remembered].'

John was a wonderful father, according to Patricia. He changed nappies and loved being around his new daughter. Sixteen months later, Hannah was born, followed in 2001 by another girl, Jaida.

In 1997 John, Patricia and Yasmin moved from John's house in North Road to a new property in Brighton's exclusive 'golden mile'. He paid $6.5 million for a large block of land directly fronting the beach. The existing house was knocked down and in its place a beautiful contemporary home was built, complete with a tennis court and basement garage.

In an interview in 2004 John commented on living in Brighton, saying, 'We find Brighton very pleasant and we are fortunate to live on the water. We can go out onto the sand in the evenings for walks with the children and watch the sun go down over the water. It's beautiful and certainly a big change from watching the sun go down over rusting cars in the creek at Broadmeadows. When I'm stressed, just looking out on the water relaxes me.'

When the empty 1700-square-metre block next door was listed on the market, John snapped it up for a reported $9 million. Properties in this waterfront enclave are tightly held, and for John, the property represented an opportunity to join the two blocks to create an expansive family home. Patricia realised John's dream in the second half of 2009, building a substantial extension, making it one of the largest estates on Brighton Beach.

Despite the happy moments in his personal life, the business front was not so rosy and John had to face the realisation that his business was flailing. 'Crazy John's was very close to going bust and John was also very close to personally going bankrupt', recalls Brendan Fleiter. 'He was being sued by two of the creditors because of personal guarantees he had given. So we were trying to hold off on those as well. We were in the Federal and Supreme Courts on those issues, and at the same time trying to do a deal with the creditors to avoid liquidation. Of course, the business survived and there was a plan in place to repay a significant amount of what was owed—about $4 million—so it was basically a process of buying time.'

It all came to a head when John was working with Brendan to prepare for the creditors' meeting that would decide the fate of Crazy John's. 'The critical point was the creditors' meeting, when those owed came together to decide if the proposal put up by the company for its future was acceptable. There was a lot of discussion among the creditors and one of the suppliers was in receivership, which complicated the process even more', says Brendan.

The night before the meeting Brendan was on the phone until midnight with some of the major creditors, trying to convince them not to vote in favour of liquidation. John's relationship with some of the creditors was essentially good, and he was confident they supported the growth of his business and would vote against liquidation. In the end John garnered the votes to move on. 'That was in May 1997. That's the day Crazy John's had its second chance', notes Brendan.

The struggle didn't end there, however. Following the survival of his business, John had to survive personally as well, because two of the business's major creditors were seeking to bankrupt him. Deals were eventually made with these creditors to accept an arrangement under the Bankruptcy Act, where John compromised rather than be placed into bankruptcy. In 1998 he made a formal deed to repay his debts and survived the bankruptcy attempts that were brought against him.

Throughout the difficulties with his company, John's business philosophy never changed. 'If you sit back and plan for too long, you never get anything started', John said. 'You can't always plan everything—in business you don't always know that one plus one will equal two. Just do something, do anything and build on that. Don't get attached to the "how", but instead hold the "why" and "what" and see where it takes you.'

But it was a lesson for John to keep a closer watch on cash flow and reorganise his senior management. Having seen Brendan in action he now wanted him to help run the business. Brendan entered Crazy John's as a director, moving into the role of managing director in 2003. After John's passing Brendan became chief executive officer of the company.

Brendan acknowledges where John's weakness lay— keeping tabs on the financial details of the business. This did not interest him as much as marketing plans or promotional ideas. 'They [his business blind spots] were financial. I reckon he never read a set of accounts. That meant he very much relied on other people for that.

'He was completely different back then. He was totally driven and refused to accept there wasn't a way out of all of the bankruptcy processes. He had the seed of a successful business, and all his instincts told him it was going to be a successful business and that one day everyone would own a mobile phone. He held onto that dream and that was the core of his success. He had the big vision', Brendan recalls.

'He never read a lease. He was a master negotiator. We'd do a deal, we knew what the objective was, and in classic entrepreneurial style he would pay more than anyone else if he thought it was strategically important. There was a lot of instinct, and rather than negotiate in the traditional way and argue about price, often the negotiations were about what other value [the other party] could provide. It was almost like the way Crazy John's customers would negotiate with us about the extras they could get if they signed up, like an accessory. That's the way John negotiated with suppliers, by getting additional benefits.

'Of course, he could be very charming and the discussions were often quite funny and joking, but underneath it all there was a commercial negotiation going on and by and large most people stuck to those commercial deals. He very much was a big-picture man and his handshake was his word.'

As John had explained in the past, he was also the first to admit that his strength was not in detail. In line with his approach there was only one way to do business—make the sales and worry about the back end later. For one store this approach just about worked, but as the business grew it started to create problems.

But John never let go of the business for a second. All the managers of all the divisions knew what was happening in every division, and all the managers were expected to meet every single staff member. Even if John's knowledge of the overall business financials was not strong, he still knew where money was being spent in the business—if someone wanted to buy a $10 chair, John would know about it. John was adamant that far from being a time-consuming irritation, the level of knowledge helped him grow the business while retaining the family culture.

When asked about his apparent control issues John said, 'If you had ten children, would you expect someone else to tell you how they are? Or would you ask each one individually and listen to what they said? You're their father, you should know what they are doing, you should play with them and put them to bed and hear what they have to say. My business is my family, and either I want to know what's going on or I don't. I either care or I don't care, and the day I don't care will be the day I leave.'

Eventually the company clawed its way back and John launched an aggressive expansion phase. He was now out to prove a point to his family—and his fallen brother—that all his hard work so far had not been for nothing.

As they say, revenge is a dish best served cold. A couple of years earlier, in 1997, a corner shop came up for sale in Brunswick. John snapped it up for $440 000. But it wasn't just any corner shop, it was the same store that he had managed for Strathfield Car Radio six years before—and Strathfield was still the tenant. 'I couldn't help myself', John said at the time. 'I bought the building prior to auction and then when Strathfield failed to exercise the option for the lease I kicked them out. I have a memory like an elephant, but I'm patient too … I bet they wish they'd paid my bonus!'

There was one other 'mistake' during this time—a foray into a broadband internet service provider, 'CrazyNet'. In 1998 broadband was the 'next big thing' to hit the technology sector and it seemed like a complimentary fit with Crazy John's core business. Broadband was still a relatively new concept at that stage and was much more an application for business users as it allowed the transmission of large files in a fraction of the time.

There was an efficiency and productivity upside that could be quantified. Non-commercial customers were not fully convinced of its usefulness or application as they generally did not need high-speed connections, instead using the internet primarily for email and internet surfing.

Crazy John's was certainly ahead of its time in trying to sell broadband to individual customers rather than business. But customers knew Crazy John's as a mobile phone provider, not as an internet provider, and it could not foster the new business opportunity. CrazyNet was shut down in 1999.

Despite all the trials and tribulations of trying to grow the business, not even John with all his optimism could have predicted just how fast Crazy John's would develop as the new millennium approached.

Chapter 8

John the brand

1999–2005

John always looked at the big picture. When Gerald passed away and he married Patricia, he made a promise that he would make the most of his life, and he extended this philosophy to the way he ran his business. With Brendan Fleiter's help, Crazy John's continued its exponential growth and brand development.

As his family was settling into their new house by Port Phillip Bay, John decided it was time for aggressive expansion. In 1997 Crazy John's lifted its retail store numbers throughout metropolitan Melbourne to ten. In 1998 John was finally recognised as a top ten Telstra mobile dealer with fifteen outlets, and by the end of 1999 the number of stores had doubled to thirty. It was in 1999 when another important figure in the Crazy John's story entered the business — Barry Hamilton, the chairman of Crazy John's.

Barry was brought into Crazy John's when it was first considering a public float on the stock exchange. He had worked as the finance director for the listed property company Hudson Conway, and it was believed his experience in helping run a publicly listed company would prove to be beneficial to the future of Crazy John's. That heralded the beginning of a close relationship between John and Barry, with Barry providing a mentoring role.

'One of John's great strengths was that he didn't think he knew everything. He had his strengths—sales, marketing and getting the best out of his staff—and he was very good at those things. But he understood that there were others better skilled than him in other aspects of running a business. I think that he realised that if the company was to get bigger, he needed other people to become involved', Barry says.

'It's all very well for John to know that that's what has to happen, but it's another to actually allow someone to come in and have a big say in his company. That's what he allowed me to do and what he allowed Brendan to do. He really listened to what other people had to say and really took it on board. That's a real strength.'

Talk of the proposed stock market float began in 1999, developing out of the tech frenzy of the same year when any company able to promote a technology angle saw its value soar. Mobile phones offered a 'tech' angle and brokers were very keen to get Crazy John's to market—and collect their broking fees, of course.

For John the approaches to list Crazy John's offered the first opportunity for him to extract some value from the business and take a down payment on his hard work. He was also genuinely surprised at the valuations of his company. He had created—he suddenly realised—a major national brand that could not only attract customers in large numbers, but also a shareholder base.

The process to prepare the listing and prospectus took about twelve months, and John's enthusiasm for turning Crazy John's from a private company into a public company—and all the constraints in terms of disclosure and accountability that went with that process—had started to wane. He was feeling doubtful about the new direction his business would take.

Brendan remembers how tempting it was to list the company. 'A lot of people at the time—there were other mobile dealers that had got out and made lots of money—were opting to take the money, and that was an option for John', he says. 'At that stage there were about thirty stores and the business was making $5 million a year of profit and it was valued at the start of 2000 at about $70 million.

'The plan at that point was to float Crazy John's on the stock exchange and John was still going to retain control. Even though he was still trying to grow the business, he was prepared to take some cash out of it. That just shows how quickly things can change. In 1997 the business was very close to going under, in 1998 John came very close to personally going under, yet by 2000 the business was independently valued at $70 million.

'At the time he was probably sitting there thinking, "I didn't realise I had a business worth $70 million". It was a lot of money back then; it still is a lot of money. To John, with his circumstances and background, going public was a very tempting option.

'There were plans to expand into Sydney, Adelaide and Brisbane, the market was booming and there were thousands of new customers each month on the Telstra network. To be told you can sell half your business and it's worth $70 million—in the context of the time, it was a pretty attractive offer.'

In the end Crazy John's did not float. Brendan was with John when he explained why he had changed his mind. 'What I recall very vividly was going to a meeting with the team of lawyers and bankers working on the float. John had spent millions on these advisers. We were standing downstairs in Bourke Street while John was having a cigarette and all these people were upstairs waiting for him to make a decision. I was standing there and John said, "I don't want to do this, so let's get back to work and get on with growing the business".

'John literally walked away from the process and a couple of million dollars he had spent on getting ready for the float and went to work the next day. All he was focused on was how he was going to keep growing the business.

'Ultimately John killed the float, but the tech wreck was a significant factor. There were delays, there were some accounting regulations that were affecting the way the prospectus was being developed and other valuation issues.'

In typical John style he moved forward quickly and made the decision to make Crazy John's the national specialist in mobile phone communications. His vision led him to announce to his company in June 2003 that Crazy John's was going to increase its presence in the market from thirty stores to 100 in the space of a year.

To achieve such fast growth, he needed to build the Crazy John's brand. Luckily, brand-building was his forte, and it would become a major factor in the growth of his business. 'If we had said let's do a business plan and look at the costs, we would have seen that the expansion was too aggressive and the numbers didn't add up, but I'm not interested in that. How do you know what will happen? The market might change—it's all unknown. If we think it's tough now, it's just going to be tougher a year from now and tougher again still a year after that. But what if we succeed? We'll be bigger and better than we ever imagined', John explained.

Around this time in the early 2000s, a few key events worked in John's favour. The biggest was that One.Tel went under owing 3000 creditors, including James Packer and Lachlan Murdoch, somewhere in the region of $600 million. In addition, Strathfield Car Radio was no longer the force it once was. In the six months leading up to June 2003, Strathfield reported a $13.2 million loss. As a consequence, between the end of 2002 and late 2003 managing director John Winstanley closed twenty-two of the company's 107 stores in an attempt to consolidate the business and control costs. Heavy stock losses, poor staffing and lacklustre product offering had seen the once-prominent brand lose its footing in the market.

They were telling times, made all the more interesting considering John and Brendan had met with Jodie Rich and Brad Keeling of One.Tel on another occasion in 1998. Jodie and Brad had asked to meet with John and Brendan, and had flown down to Melbourne to discuss buying the business. John was not seriously interested in selling the business, but the poetic justice of the situation was too good to refuse. Brad had run Strathfield Car Radio during the early 1990s—at the time when Strathfield offered him $5000 to disappear from its street in Brunswick. John was interested to see how the offer had increased; however, he never did find out because the meeting lasted only ten minutes. Despite saying they wanted to buy the business, Jodie and Brad would not make an offer. Instead, they wanted John to say how much he wanted.

Brendan recalls that Jodie leaned across the table and said, 'Have a bit of chocolate'. 'I said, "I didn't come here to eat chocolate—either you want to buy the business or you don't. If you do then tell us how much you are going to pay for it so we can understand, if not then piss off".' They pissed off.

With his competitors suffering, John took on a much more aggressive approach to brand development. He recognised he needed to create wacky ambush branding exercises to catapult Crazy John's into the national consciousness, and he had the utmost confidence in his tactics.

A perfect opportunity for a stunt arose on the morning of Thursday 14 August 2003. John was listening to the radio while he shaved when a promo for a reality television show on Channel Nine called *The Block* came on. The show was a competition between four couples to each renovate a run-down apartment that would then be auctioned. The winner would be whoever achieved the highest price when each apartment was auctioned.

Hosted by popular celebrity landscaper Jamie Durie, the program followed the progress of the couples in their bid to renovate apartments in the Sydney suburb of Bondi. The apartments became home for each couple as they renovated over three months on a tight budget. After the auction, the competitors could keep whatever money was made above the reserve price, with the winning couple also pocketing an extra $100000. The auction was to be held just two days later on Saturday in Sydney.

Always keen to build the Crazy John's profile, John thought it would be the perfect stunt. 'It just hit me', said John. 'Why couldn't Crazy John [the mascot] go to the auction and bid for an apartment?' However, he did not want it to be just a stunt—he wanted to genuinely buy one of the apartments.

The next two days were spent frantically arranging the legalities, finding someone to wear the mascot outfit, and locating a lawyer that was able to fly to Sydney at very short notice. The stage was soon set with Crazy John's lawyer, Michael Muir, and the mascot flying to Sydney to attend the auction on the Saturday.

The program was a huge hit for Channel Nine, and at Roscoe Street in Bondi, where the program was filmed, the auction day for the first two apartments resembled a carnival. The street was jam-packed with 3000 onlookers, including interstate viewers who had travelled especially for the auction, security guards, circling television helicopters and neighbours holding their own sausage sizzles. It was also a branding dream, as the crowd was bombarded by advertising and merchandise including Toyota hats, Commonwealth Bank water, real estate agent balloons and even Toyota writing its logo in the sky.

John picked the moment superbly. He had authorised a budget of $1 million to ensure the purchase of one of the apartments and Michael was confident that they wouldn't be leaving empty-handed. He said in a newspaper interview that the plan was to bid for the ground floor garden apartment belonging to 'the boys'—Gavin Atkins and Warren Sonin. 'The unit will be tenanted', Michael explained. 'We'll be selecting a charity and the proceeds will go to that charity. We thought it was the best one on *The Block*.'[1] The other apartment upstairs, owned by Amity Dry and Phil Rankine, was to be auctioned first.

Amity and Phil's apartment sold for $655 000. Then the sight of the more than two metres tall Crazy John's mascot lent a somewhat circus-like air to the proceedings, as Gav and Waz's, as they came to be known, auction began to unfold. The mascot attracted plenty of laughs from the thousands amassed and the bidding was spirited, especially when the price was pushed up by a failed bidder from the first auction.

The Crazy John's charm worked, and the mascot success-fully snapped up the apartment for $670 000. Although the overall winning apartment sold for $751 000 the following day, John was true to his word and leased out the apartment for two years, with all rental proceeds going to a children's charity.

He sold it two years later as the Sydney property market was booming—recouping a hefty profit. That was a typical win–win outcome for John, with the whole idea turned around in just two days.

More than three million viewers tuned in to see the final episode of *The Block*, which represented about half of Australia's television audience at that time. Channel Nine reported that the figures made the show the most successful Australian television show ever, and with the Crazy John's mascot involved, the brand was able to reach millions of potential customers in addition to the thousands who turned out on the day. Crucially, it enabled Crazy John's to penetrate into other states where there had been little presence previously.

Reaching millions of viewers through television was a strategy John also employed when it came to another one of his passions—sport. Recognising that he could benefit by mixing his two loves, sport and business, he began to see how beneficial for his business it might be to throw some financial weight behind various sporting organisations.

In Victoria sport on television is largely driven by Australian Rules football. Practically a religion in Melbourne, the Australian Football League (AFL) attracts both men and women, and John saw it as a strong branding strategy. 'It's a fallacy to say that women don't watch sport', said John. 'About half a million people watch *The Footy Show* and ratings indicate that more than half are women in the eighteen to thirty-five year old age range.'

By advertising at a football ground and sponsoring different clubs he could target his brand directly to the hearts and minds of his audience. Interestingly, he sent out a letter to every club in the AFL offering sponsorship, but it was only the Hawthorn Football Club that responded. So he originally sponsored the Hawks, and from there went on to support the Collingwood and St Kilda football clubs. Crazy John's is still one of Collingwood's major sponsors. But the club John threw most of his weight behind was Richmond, who he had followed passionately from a young age. He poured tens of thousands of dollars into Richmond in the mid 2000s, and at one stage even expressed a desire to become the Tigers' president.

In 2007 John's strategies made the headlines when he offered $1 million to any player who could kick ten goals in the AFL Grand Final. He extended the offer to the Sydney-based National Rugby League (NRL), offering a similar amount to any player who could score five tries in the NRL grand final.

Crazy John's sponsored a few different NRL clubs: the Melbourne Storm, the Penrith Panthers, the Sydney Roosters and the Canterbury Bulldogs. In another NRL campaign, John had a plan to take ownership of NRL club Manly Sea Eagles. The plan provoked anger after he devised a scheme that involved players changing their name by deed poll to Crazy John. Crazy John's sponsors the AFL *Footy Show* on Channel Nine and also sponsored the NRL *Footy Show*.

John's exploits extended to other sports, too. Past sponsorships include Gymnastics Victoria, the Anthony Mundine versus Danny Green Boxing Match in 2007, various kickboxing events, Lamborghini team racing and the *Jack of All Trades* television show on Channel Nine. Crazy John's also has the naming rights to the Surf Life Saving Championships in Queensland.

Explaining his reasons for sport sponsorship John said, 'I love sport. I love the competition and the camaraderie of it. It makes sense to be involved in sport from a sponsorship perspective, not only because it fits the company culture and objectives, but it makes commercial sense, too. Millions of people watch sport week in and week out. They see the Crazy John's name and logo week in and week out. It's all about staying in the hearts and minds of your target audience. And my target audience is watching sport. If they are having a great day out enjoying the game or if they are with friends watching TV and having a great time, they will associate my brand with those positive feelings — that's good for business.'

In 2003 John approached well-known racehorse owner and advertising guru John Singleton and asked him to rename his horse Zagalia to Crazy John's. Singleton laughed and said, 'Mate, you are going to have Harvey Norman coming second, Crazy John's third followed by Coca-Cola'. John ended up sponsoring a race in the 2003 Spring Racing Carnival, but was more interested in taking a larger piece of the corporate pie by sponsoring the Melbourne Cup. In 2004 he hatched a plan to win the naming rights to the famous horse race, but ruffled a few feathers among the racing fraternity in the process. In the end, Crazy John's did not go on to sponsor Australia's most illustrious horse race, but the attempt did indicate the boldness of John's ideas.

John's willingness to think creatively certainly paved the way for sport sponsorship deals in Australia. Before Crazy John's involvement with the AFL, no telecommunications company had thought twice about sponsoring the sport or advertising at the grounds.

John also realised that there was more than one way to advertise — one cost money and the other did not. The ability to make Crazy John's appear a bigger company than it really was did not come cheaply — John was spending $5 million a year on sports sponsorship alone in Australia — but the controversies created free publicity that helped Crazy John's stay in the public consciousness.

Eddie McGuire remembers how their friendship evolved after the initial meetings through Triple M and the contentious schemes John was involved in. 'After we met we did a lot of things together, like Crazy John's sponsoring *The Footy Show*, and we developed a friendship that moved into a phase of mutual respect and trust. We also had a lot of fun along the way, like [*The Footy Show* breaking the story] of renaming Subiaco Oval in Perth Crazy John's Oval.'

The Subiaco idea was perhaps John's most controversial scheme. One morning in July 2003 the Australian division of a London-based sports marketing company, which had been instructed to sell the naming rights to the oval, sent an email asking whether Crazy John's would be interested in purchasing the rights to Subiaco Oval. John proposed to change the name of Perth's Subiaco Oval to Crazy John's Stadium.

John read the message that morning, punched the number into his phone and threw it to Brendan, saying, 'Do the deal'. By that afternoon, Crazy John's had issued a proposal and a deal was formulated to pay $5 million over five years for naming rights plus $500 000 for junior development. The fact that redevelopment of the ground had left the Western Australian Football Commission with a $30 million debt certainly meant that a sponsorship deal was a step in the right direction.

However, football fans in Western Australia fiercely love the iconic Subiaco Oval, and there was much vocal resistance from locals who did not take too kindly to the possibility of their hallowed turf being renamed — especially by some east-coast outfit called Crazy John's with its disfigured cartoon character as a mascot. The mayor at the time, Tony Costa, didn't like the idea either, and it seemed there was no way that the Subiaco Municipal Oval was going to sell its naming rights.

In addition, Western Australians had little knowledge of Crazy John's, but they soon did as the marketing company caused a frenzy by leaking the story to the media, and John was accused of orchestrating the response for maximum publicity.

The issue was further complicated by the heritage listing of the entrance gates to the ground, which prominently displayed the words 'Subiaco Oval'. If the gates remained, future signing could be difficult because the ground would continue to be recognised by its original name.

In the end the deal fell through. A conflict of interest arose due to a clash with the sponsor of the West Coast Eagles, Optus, whose home stadium is Subiaco Oval. The commission thought it could sell the rights, but it could actually only sell indoor signage. Had the deal gone ahead, Crazy John's would have had no outside signage, no directional signage, no map changes and no street directory changes. The media would be 'encouraged' to refer to the ground as Crazy John's Stadium, but even then the internal signage could only be displayed when the West Coast Eagles were not playing. The commission pulled out as it couldn't deliver what was in the agreement.

It was not a wasted exercise, though, as the publicity generated plenty of buzz in Perth. Although they were disappointed to miss out on the naming rights, Crazy John's was able to leverage the media attention and open eight stores in Perth with a strong corporate sales team. Again, it was a win–win situation.

A couple of years later in 2005, John ruffled a few more feathers with another radical scheme. He unveiled a design for a $40 million tower in the shape of a phone, which was to house his communications empire, retail shops and 166 luxury two-, three- and four-bedroom apartments spread over thirty-four levels. The high-rise would be based at the Crazy John's headquarters site in City Road, South Melbourne, and it would feature a giant keypad and display screen, 'end' and 'send' buttons, and be topped with a rooftop antenna. John had high hopes that it would become a Melbourne landmark. 'Every country has a building of some sort. Sydney has the Opera House—why not this for Melbourne?' he told the *Herald Sun*. 'I just want Melbourne to stand out—that's the idea behind it.'[2]

The permits were granted for the 110-metre building that he wanted to call Crazy John's House, but he did not gain approval to incorporate the latest, more radical alterations to the plans, so he decided to scrap the whole thing.

John's penchant for finding novel adaptations of business paradigms was not just restricted to advertising. A classic example was during early 2003. The management team decided a store was needed in the Sydney CBD and the managers were told to be on the lookout for suitable premises. The New South Wales state manager soon identified a potential outlet in George Street at the intersection of Hunter Street. It was a great location because there was a lot of passing traffic and it was opposite a flagship Optus store. John and Brendan were in Melbourne and flew to Sydney to have a look.

They walked into Trumps—a hairdressing salon packed with women in various stages of transformation—and introduced themselves to the owner, a rather fraught-looking woman. There had been some correspondence between Crazy John's and the salon's owner, so she knew who John and Brendan were, but she was a little taken aback that they were now standing in front of her.

In the ensuing conversation, John and Brendan discovered that she not only owned the business, but that her family owned the whole building. After discussing their intention to take over the premises, which the owner had indicated to

Brendan she was open to, they explained Crazy John's plans for rapid expansion and their desire to move quickly. As a show of good faith and Crazy John's commitment to lease her premises Brendan transferred $5000 into her account on the spot via her EFTPOS machine. The owner remarked that she would most likely get a query from the bank about a $5000 transaction.

After five minutes of discussion and reassurance that the lawyers would iron out the details, they shook hands and the deal was done. The lawyers sorted out the details, and Crazy John's was in the location within a couple of months.

By finding situations where the normal rules of business do not apply, Crazy John's was able to secure a prime site in the Sydney CBD and to have it opened and operating in the time it would have normally taken just to negotiate the contract. And it acquired signage for the entire building at the same time. All parties were happy with the final deal, and Trumps moved to a new location upstairs.

John was positive that seeking out these sorts of opportunities would make a huge difference to the success and rapid growth of the business. 'I never broke the rules, but if there were rules I would certainly see how far I could bend them', he said. 'I never worried about what the "right way" was. The truth is, in most instances there is an "accepted way", which may or may not be the best way. I say challenge everything, challenge the assumptions of your industry and find better ways of doing business that benefit the most people. When you hear phrases like, "But we've always done it that way", take a good look at how it's being done and try something new and see what happens. I know I upset a lot of people in the early days with this way of thinking, but I also changed the industry as a result, and that saved customers thousands of dollars.'

John kept a tight fist on all marketing strategies and campaigns. Without exception, he oversaw all advertising before it was released and he was very strict with this policy. He usually wrote the copy and created the concepts himself, and he possessed an uncanny ability to know instinctively what would work. In another example of the free publicity attracted by the maniacal Crazy John's character, at one point SANE Australia, the national mental health charity, requested the mascot be discontinued as it disrespected the mentally ill. The charity lodged a formal complaint with the health minister, who convened a board to examine the accusations. Crazy John's was asked to provide samples of its logo and advertising material. The board found in favour of Crazy John's, concluding that the mobile phone retailer had not overstepped the mark.

Another way that John built his brand was by heading up regular roadshows with Brendan to personally visit all of his stores around Australia. Not only did it mean that management could stay in touch with the grassroots of the business, but such a positive step by the boss might equate to better results because of John's commitment to his staff. It also flattened the management structure, meaning greater communication between those making sales and those making the big decisions.

John believed it was the company's responsibility to ensure everyone was included and visited, regardless of how remote they might be. It gave him the chance to really meet everyone. The roadshow went outside the major centres, visiting Cairns even though there was only one store there. As Brendan pointed out, 'If we didn't visit the more remote stores, they would have every right to feel left out and marginalised, and that was not going to happen—everyone is important'.

It was not a formal roadshow either; it was mainly about having fun and saying hello in an informal environment. For example, John and Brendan flew to Adelaide to go bowling with all the staff from the seven Adelaide stores. A week later they flew to Perth and took all the staff go-karting. Crazy John's has also hired Luna Park in Melbourne and Sydney, and invited all the staff and their families for an exclusive Crazy John's night out with free rides and fairy floss. As these events were social, staff were relaxed and more likely to feel confident enough to discuss things openly, rather than hearing them second hand, filtered through a couple of layers of management who could be protecting their patch, driving their own agendas or covering up for their own failings. The aim of these events was to take the corporate culture to a more personal level where staff became friends and competition was healthy.

John said at the time, 'It keeps the business human. All too often, especially in growing businesses, the head of the company disappears from view. As soon as that happens, he or she will start to lose touch and I have no intention of doing that. Crazy John's is a retail army and I want everyone to feel comfortable approaching me—whether they work in Melbourne or Mackay.'

The phenomenal growth and success of Crazy John's did not alter John's attitude towards money. It was never his main motivator and he was never attached to his wealth. John firmly believed his neutral feelings towards money stemmed from early conditioning by his parents, who were more interested in his integrity and whether he was being a good husband and father to his children.

John recalled, 'If I am talking with my father and telling him about something that's happened or some high-profile person I've met or a deal that's gone ahead that's made money, he never fails to remind me about the important things in life. They are happy for my success but it doesn't affect them, instead they ask me what I've done for other people today. Or what have I put into my family or whether I've made time for my kids. They are the things they respect.'

Ali and Nezaket did not want to give their children the impression that money was scarce or alternatively that it was plentiful; they wanted it to never be an issue. They had a completely different mindset from their Turkish immigrant friends, who, believing they could only stay in the country legally for two years, would work hard, save every cent and then return home to Turkey. 'Our parents didn't think that was right because these families were scrimping on everything', says Ayse. 'The kids were deprived of even the tiniest treats, like bars of chocolate, so that that the family could go home with as much money as possible. With us, our parents were still saving, but they never deprived us of anything.

'There were so many things then that parents weren't aware of about the psychological development of children, and I think mum was a bit ahead of her time. We would all get pocket money, none of us paid board or had jobs to help with the bills, so our parents took care of everything for us. I was the baby so I would get $1.50 a day. That was fifty cents more than my friends and it was more than I ever needed. It took care of recess and snacks and lunchtime, and usually I had the extra fifty cents left over. Gerald and John each got $20 every couple of days.'

The family did not necessarily have much, but Ali and Nezaket felt it was essential for the kids to have sufficient money that they never thought about it. Nezaket would often leave little piles of change and a few notes around the house to see how the children would react. It was her way of teaching them that money wasn't a big deal. The got used to seeing money around the house, and they never moved it or took it.

According to Ayse, 'They didn't want us to look at other people and want what they had. The logic was that if we had all we needed we wouldn't have any jealousy or bad feelings toward other people because of what they had. And it worked—we didn't care about those things because we knew we could get them if we really wanted by saving up our pocket money. They wanted to get rid of any nasty thought that could have been embedded in our minds at a young age because they believed that the early years of our life were crucial to how we would think as adults.'

John never displayed any early signs of entrepreneurial spirit so often seen in other self-made millionaires. For example, Richard Branson was always inventing new ways to add to his pocket money, whereas John's approach was to give it away. Ayse vividly remembers John throwing change away in the street. She says, 'He would take all his copper money and just throw it away'.

As for his work, John took a similar approach. Accumulating wealth was simply a nice side effect of the more personally challenging role of being the best he could be, improving the business, creating clever marketing campaigns and making the business grow. He said, 'Even when I was building the business and it was going well it wasn't what drove me. I had made my first million long before I even moved out of home. If I was driven by money, surely I would have moved out and got a flashy car, but I didn't. I was more than happy at home. My parents would feed me and support me—I lived like a king.'

Patricia offers a little more insight into John's attitude to wealth. 'John liked to know that he'd got the best of what was available without necessarily using it. If I wasn't sure what to buy, he'd just say to get the best one, but then not mention it to anyone. He might not have even used it. He just got comfort knowing that he had the best. We have beautiful homes and we went away every year with the kids, which was probably one of our greatest luxuries. We went to Europe and saw places we hadn't been to before. In 2001 we went to Istanbul in Turkey. John had [not been back] to Turkey, so that was fun. But we never went without the kids—it was always a family affair.'

As John became more successful he began to be recognised more often by the public, which made some things difficult for the family. Patricia recalls that even just going out locally for dinner became an issue. 'John's profile grew so big that his face became a brand in its own right. We'd stopped going out for dinner publicly—you just couldn't. If we ever went out on our own, people on the street would come and talk to him, which you can't get angry about because he's such a nice guy and he touched so many people in many ways. It's the symptom of having a profile.

'People who have a high profile find very private places to get together. When we were down at Portsea, if John ever had a coffee with Eddie McGuire, it was always at the back of a little café at the Portsea shops. Never in Sorrento, which was too busy.'

John's brand was so huge that in 2003 Crazy John's grew to a national network of 100 stores, turning over about $200 million for a profit of over $20 million. Personally, in 2003 John was named the richest person in Australia under forty, topping *BRW* magazine's Young Rich List with $200 million. A year later he debuted on *BRW*'s Rich 200 list with a fortune of $300 million and an annual turnover of $200 million.

As John's wealth increased, he discovered a major weakness for luxury cars. In 2004 he bought himself a Lamborghini Murcielago, and alternated between this and his Mercedes Benz SL55 AMG. Patricia's preferences were somewhat less extravagant. She alternated between a four-wheel-drive Lexus and a BMW convertible.

In 2005 John gave something back to his parents. True to his promise to return the $15 000 that he borrowed when he was twenty-six, he went one better—he built them a brand-new house in Greenvale. It was a gesture to thank them for all their support over the years. Following this, he took further steps to secure the future of his family by establishing Ilhan Holdings Pty Ltd, his family investment company.

Yet despite the growth, success and money, he always had a gorilla looking over his shoulder.

Chapter 9

Becoming free

2004–2007

There was always a significant other in John's life: Telstra. The telecommunications giant played a vital role in both his personal and business dealings, from the early days of having just one store to employing John's future wife Patricia. Telstra was the gorilla looking over his shoulder, and John found that the constant supervision stunted his entrepreneurial drive and creative spirit. The telco watched especially closely when Crazy John's began to experience immense growth and success.

The relationship was somewhat of a paradox: Telstra would set the guidelines and John would do his utmost to bend them. John had a clear idea of what was right and wrong, due to his religious background and strong family values, but when it came to business, he either found rules that could be bent a little, or games where the rules did not apply.

For example, Telstra had very specific advertising guidelines about promoting phone deals, but John constantly pushed the boundaries. He always managed to get away with it until one occasion in 1998 when he was prosecuted for misleading advertising. He took the action very seriously, so much so that he hired prominent Queen's Counsel Robert Richter to defend the company.

According to Barry Hamilton, who joined Crazy John's in 1999 as the chairman, Telstra thought John was crazy. '[Telstra] thought he was difficult to deal with and completely unpredictable. It worried them that they couldn't get a fix on him. I was in one meeting where we talked and we weren't getting our way, and John could see that what Telstra were putting up was really bad for his business.

'He just pointed his finger at this particular Telstra senior manager and said, "Look, I came into this business with absolutely nothing and I'm happy to go out with nothing, but this is not going to look good for you". And he just looked at the Telstra executive, and the executive went to water. The next day Telstra came back with a super deal. Because they couldn't read him they thought, geez, this guy's unpredictable, he might just scuttle the whole thing. And so that really worked to his advantage sometimes.

'On the other hand he got along really well with some Telstra executives, and they realised he could deliver. In the early days it obviously suited them to push John's business forward, because it was when the Global System for Mobile communications (GSM) networks for mobile phones first came out, and John had the ability to really push it hard and give them results. They probably thought that they could bring his business to an end any time they liked, but at the moment he was doing some great work and that's fantastic.'

Ultimately, if Crazy John's was doing well, so was Telstra, because all of John's connections were to its network. He knew that he was one of Telstra's best dealers, but Telstra couldn't control him. In the early years John was fiercely loyal to the telco and felt sure that this would pay off eventually. When Optus and Vodafone entered the market, and then later other carriers, many of them approached him with open chequebooks and appealing offers, but he always said no.

'I'm a great believer in bringing things down to the basics and bringing things back to the simplicity of life', explained John. 'At the time many dealers were opting for multi-carrier agreements, including Strathfield Car Radio, but it just didn't seem right to me. It was like me having three wives—how was I going to keep all three happy? It would never work. If you bring it back down to life and people, you always get the answer. I am adamant I made the right choice [to stay with one carrier] and I think Telstra respected that decision.'

But Crazy John's chief executive Brendan Fleiter recalls that tension was always there. 'Crazy John's was trying to extract the maximum value from Telstra, and Telstra was aiming to pay the minimum commissions possible to attract and retain customers', he says. Barry agrees: 'He got bigger and bigger, and [Telstra] got to the stage where they had a sort of love–hate relationship with him. They couldn't let him go, but they hated the idea that they were making him bigger and giving him more power.'

Another court battle took place in 2003. It was against Crazy Ron's, the store Ron Bakir had opened two doors down from a Crazy John's store in Mermaid Beach on the Gold Coast. There were now sixteen Crazy Ron's stores and the business had expanded into Melbourne and Sydney. John decided it was time to sue, spending more than $1 million on a four-day trial.

Discussing the case and why he had waited so long to take action, John said, 'I know some people would say that I waited too long to do something about it, but I didn't have a choice. I had to save the business first. I never had any intention of letting him get away with it. It was all just timing. I regret I couldn't have handled it earlier but it's just the way it turned out.'

In his findings Justice James Allsop agreed that Crazy Ron's had traded with a name and image that was substantially identical or deceptively similar to that of its competition. He said, 'There was direct evidence of people confusing and indeed mistaking one shop for another after hearing or seeing the other's advertising. Some customers on the phone were adamant that the stores they heard advertising as Crazy Ron's stores were Crazy John's stores.' Crazy Ron was forced to change his name.

After the verdict even broadcaster Alan Jones weighed into the case. Jones ran the story over two days on his 2GB show, arguing that the verdict was unfair, uncompetitive and a typical tall poppy approach to a young entrepreneur. One of his arguments was that there were 347 businesses in Australia with the prefix Crazy. However, those other companies do not sell mobile phones, which is what made all the difference.

John denied the similarity between his and any of the other 'Crazy' businesses, and argued that Crazy Ron's had deliberately tried to profit from his hard work. 'I used to push the boundaries for sure and it landed me in some hot water a few times', he said. 'I was aggressively advertising, piggybacking other campaigns for maximum exposure, but I never deliberately damaged a brand or stole ideas. I never copied someone else's advertising ideas or their look and feel. Although I ambushed a few Telstra campaigns, which granted they didn't like, Telstra always benefited from my success anyway because of the nature of the relationship. This was different; it was a blatant attempt to profit from my business and hard work. I can be very stubborn—especially when I believe I have right on my side. In this case I had right on my side and I refused to budge.'

The paradox between Telstra and John was constantly tested and the two clashed on many occasions. The result was a few minor disputes between 2000 and 2002, and a major, highly publicised battle that began in 2004. 'At that time Crazy John's was Telstra's mobile dealer of the year and David Moffatt had just come on as Group Managing Director [of Telstra Consumer Marketing & Channels. Previously he had been Telstra's Chief Financial Officer and Group Managing Director, Finance and Administration]', explains Brendan.

'[David] certainly had a different way of resolving legal issues', comments Barry. 'My experience of him was that he didn't negotiate with anyone, he simply adopted a position and nothing was going to shift him from that position. He would probably say the same thing about John. It was a relationship that was the most poisoned commercial relationship [between John and David Moffatt] I have ever seen.

'We'd have a five-year deal, yet every twelve months Telstra would have us back at the negotiating table. [It was the same] with Moffatt. He [had us] back at the negotiating table at the end of 2003—and he went about negotiating the deal in a different way. Normally we'd sit down and talk about it, but this time it was done under a different scenario. Essentially Telstra claimed that Crazy John's had been paid during 2003 about $12 million more than we were entitled to in commissions.'

David Moffatt and former Group Managing Director Ted Pretty were named as authorising and negotiating the percentage of commission to be paid to Crazy John's, which was typically between five and eleven per cent in the industry.

In January 2004 Telstra demanded the money be paid back, and that the payment was required within five days or Telstra would terminate Crazy John's dealership agreement. However, the amount the telco demanded had been unexpectedly increased to $21.3 million. 'This developed into a massive dispute that arose out of one of John's handshake deals with Ted Pretty at Telstra', explains Brendan. 'Basically John had a gun held at his head: pay the $21 million or agree to the new terms.'

As requested, Crazy John's paid the money and a month later counter-sued Telstra for precisely $21 283 642.61, paid to Telstra 'involuntarily and under protest'.[1] Crazy John's claimed that a verbal agreement made with Ted Pretty had been instrumental in Crazy John's agreeing to the latest arrangement with Telstra and that demanding the repayment of commission was not in accordance with the deal negotiated.

In addition, Crazy John's questioned the validity of Telstra's commissions system, stating it could not produce accurate data, and hence could not prove Crazy John's owed any money. Crazy John's alleged Telstra's commission system was fundamentally flawed. John reacted badly to the way the negotiation was carried out by Telstra. Both had done extremely well out of the relationship, but as Brendan notes, 'There are always going to be issues when you have a small entrepreneurial private business dealing with an 800-pound gorilla. For John, it was a matter of principle. He didn't care who they were, he believed he was right and he would fight them to the end to prove his point.'

John said at the time, 'We still have a working relationship. Sure I'm disappointed that after a thirteen-year relationship we have to resort to court proceedings, but given the significant sums involved we had no choice. I believe that my case is valid and I can't just accept something that I don't believe is right just because I've had a long relationship. In a strong and healthy relationship both parties stand up for themselves and that's all that we are doing. I'm loyal to my business and that's just common sense.'

There were three different court cases between Crazy John's and Telstra from 2004 to 2007. The major case was heard in the Federal Court, but the only case that did not settle and went to judgement was a case in the Supreme Court. It involved the entitlement of Crazy John's to open retail outlets without Telstra's permission. Telstra lost that case and was ordered to pay Crazy John's costs.

The major case heard in the Federal Court had been running since 2004. The trial commenced in October 2006 and lasted for three weeks, at which time a settlement was reached. It had a huge impact on the senior members of Crazy John's—John, Barry and Brendan—who were still trying to operate the business while at the same time fighting the biggest company in Australia in court.

The pivotal moment in the trial was when John, Barry and Brendan each had to take the stand and face days of questioning by Telstra's legal team. 'It was terribly stressful', Barry recalls. 'I mean it took a long time to get to that court case—something like two-and-a-half years. All the way along we thought we had a pretty good case, but as it gets closer and you know that you are going to have to go on the stand. Telstra brought in a really top barrister, a fellow called Allan Myers, who has a big reputation in Melbourne, to act for them. We knew it was going to be pretty tough.

'We had to go first—we were the plaintiffs—and for whatever reason I was chosen to go first. I was on the stand for over two days, John was on the stand for probably a day and Brendan was probably on the stand for three days. The whole time you are getting grilled by the other side. They just pick on everything they can and try to make out that the case we're making is either false or that we don't believe in it ourselves, or it's just not truthful and all that sort of thing. It's very stressful and you've just got to answer the questions. We were advised, "Don't try to put your slant on things, just answer the question, don't try come back at him, don't let him get you riled".'

John's sister Ayse recalls his thoughts at the time. 'He never once thought Telstra was too big, had too much money to take on in court. He always believed he was right—every time he ran in rather than ran away from it. He'd say, "That was something new I was about to learn about. If I'm doing well that's why they find me a threat". He always thought, "No-one is going to stop me".'

Back in the courtroom, it was Telstra's turn to testify. 'As soon as we'd finished and they'd done us over as much as they could, it was their turn to [take the stand]', says Barry. 'We thought this might be a time where they'd want to talk about a settlement.

'Once you go into the box [the opposing lawyers] can ask anything they like, so Telstra's executives didn't really want to get in the box as they didn't know where [the questioning] was going to go. The difference was that they were managers, whereas John was a proprietor—it was John's business. These guys had reputations to think about and they had ambitions within Telstra, and they didn't want to go into a court case and be placed into a box where they could come out of it looking badly. So they agreed that we'd talk settlement before they [took the stand], which was good on the one hand, but we would have loved them to go in the box and experience what we'd had to go through.'

The case settled midway through the trial with a multimillion-dollar payment to Crazy John's. In hindsight Barry said it was a court case that Crazy John's really had to go through. 'Even though it was a distraction, it galvanised our thinking too, to say that we could not live with Telstra anymore. What Telstra was trying to do was something that would have had a long-term adverse effect on the business. The Crazy John's business was set up to operate in a certain way, and they wanted to work in a different manner.'

In an interview with *The Age* newspaper in September 2005, John said he was 'fed up with Telstra's bullying' and that Telstra was no longer competitive. 'We need the flexibility to deliver what our customers want so we can respond better than we now can to the competition we face.'[2] Barry agrees. 'The litigation made us realise that he had to move away from Telstra. We had to make our own business and live or die by those plans. We had to be a better business and thought we could do it. If John was still alive, he could and would have done it.'

John wanted Crazy John's to become a more mature business. His plan was for the business to become an MVNO—a mobile virtual network operator. The MVNO strategy meant that Crazy John's would buy network capacity from one of the major mobile carriers in Australia—Telstra, Optus or Vodafone. In 2005 John and Brendan travelled to the United States, Europe and Asia researching MVNO operations. Vodafone Australia was the carrier John wanted to sign with.

It also required executing a different business model, so with the court case finally settled John was ready to move on with his future plans for the company. He planned for these to take effect when the exclusive contract with Telstra ran out in June 2007. For Crazy John's, becoming an MVNO meant it would service its own customers. Instead of receiving a commission for connecting customers to the Telstra network, which meant billing and any issues were handed straight over, Crazy John's would be the only point of contact for the customer. It required significant infrastructure and billing systems, which ultimately would prove very attractive to Vodafone later down the track.

In July 2007 Crazy John's went live as an MVNO. It invested about $50 million to set up the systems, and entered into a new relationship with Vodafone, leaving Telstra behind after fifteen years. Brendan recalls the new liaison was a huge step forward. 'I remember when the Telstra court case was on in 2006—it was a difficult time for us all to run both the business and a major court case. John had so much at stake in that court case and yet he was quite philosophical about things. He had made more money than he knew what to do with, he could buy anything he wanted. When it came to that court case he was fighting for what he thought was right. His lifestyle wasn't going to change as a result of anything that happened in court.

'John was just so excited about the association with Vodafone. We had a meeting in Sydney with the global boss of Vodafone and John talked about the Crazy John's brand and how he saw opportunities for it to expand overseas and keep growing. He was gratified to have a partner who was finally backing him rather than fighting with them. In his mind that was a great relief.'

At the same time the new business model was a big risk for John. Not only was the financial outlay a significant investment putting the company in debt, but for the first time in the company's history he really was on his own. The fact that the prior business model was already a success and that John wanted to move in a different direction was a huge responsibility for him to shoulder, but he was determined to make it work. Ultimately, he believed this independence would be better for the long-term future of the company.

The pressure was on to get the MVNO business up and running. Following the evening meal with his family he would start working again, calling individual area and store managers every night right up until midnight to ensure they were on track. It was almost as if he was starting out all over again.

Barry remembers that although it was common for John to call colleagues at midnight, he did not notice John acting particularly stressed, despite it being an anxious time for him. 'I'm sure that John's stress levels must have been greater. Crazy John's went from a business that didn't require debt and just received the commissions from Telstra every month, to a system where you had a lot of bank debt because of the infrastructure and systems that were put into place. It was a completely different business, a much more complex business, and it must have been stressful for him. It was stressful for all of us, it must have been especially stressful for him, but I don't think it was really evident. He was really buoyant and optimistic, and staff probably didn't see much change in him.

'I would have thought he was driving them in the same way as he was before. I don't think there were any greater occurrences of outbursts at this time than previously. You know, he'd had a lot of stressful times before. He might have said that the stress that he had when he first started the business, when he borrowed money from his parents and then didn't know how he was going to pay them back was more stressful than, "How am I going to pay a bank back?" So I think he'd been through a lot in his early days and he probably had the experience to withstand some of that.'

As if the David and Goliath battle was not enough, there was yet another battle that was being waged at the same time. It stemmed from an event involving his youngest daughter, and would provide him with the ideal opportunity to throw his weight and money in a different direction.

Chapter 10

Food for thought

2005-2006

In mid 2005 John and Patricia went away for the weekend to the internationally renowned Lake House guesthouse in Daylesford in Victoria's spa district. The reason for the break was to spend some time together and discuss the health crisis affecting their third daughter, Jaida. They had only recently fully come to terms with the fact that Jaida had been diagnosed with a potentially life-threatening illness—severe anaphylaxis to tree nuts. This type of allergy means that sufferers, mostly children, have a physical reaction to nuts, such as almonds, cashews, walnuts and hazelnuts, even if exposed to the smallest amount. Tree nut allergies are different from peanut allergies, but both symptoms are the same, the worst reaction being severe anaphylaxis. In practical terms it meant that if Jaida accidentally ate the wrong food, she could die within minutes without medical intervention or self-medication.

Anaphylaxis occurs when the airways rapidly constrict, which can lead to respiratory failure and arrest. Urgent medical attention is required and the anaphylaxis is treated with adrenaline, which prevents worsening of the airway constriction. Many sufferers carry an EpiPen containing adrenaline that must be injected should an attack occur.

The anaphylaxis diagnosis followed an episode in early 2003 when Jaida's face became acutely swollen and she was rushed to hospital. The family had been staying at the Como Hotel in South Yarra while the air-conditioning units in their house were being relocated. John had opened a jar of mixed nuts and ate a selection before Jaida walked into the room. John started tickling her and kissing her face, when suddenly it swelled up. Patricia called the hotel doctor, who took one look at her and said she had had an allergic reaction. 'We got such a fright. She swelled up like an alien', Patricia recalls.

Jaida was two at the time and nuts were common in the Ilhan household. There had been no family history of food allergies, even in the extended family. In fact nuts are used widely in Turkish cooking and John had grown up with them. In retrospect, what was even more frightening for John and Patricia was that if Jaida had eaten any of the nuts lying around, rather than been indirectly exposed, the consequences could easily have been tragic.

'We discovered that it was me', John told *The Age* in an interview in 2006. 'I ate some peanuts that morning, I gave her a kiss and her whole face came up... luckily for us it was from my kiss rather than her eating some nuts.'[1] John and Patricia rushed Jaida to the Royal Children's Hospital, not knowing what was wrong with their daughter. Within hours of admission to the emergency department, she was given an antihistamine, and the Ilhans' lifestyle changed forever.

The next step in dealing with Jaida's medical challenge was to book an appointment at the Allergy Clinic at the Royal Children's Hospital for further tests. That was when John and Patricia received their next shock—the waiting list for the clinic was almost fifteen months. Neither could quite believe it, especially as they now felt they were dealing with a life and death situation on a daily basis when it came to Jaida's diet.

Very quickly John and Patricia were being introduced to the problems confronting the whole food allergy community. They began to take notice of the problems with food labelling and how ill-prepared the restaurant industry was for dealing with allergies. John believed it was only a matter of time before a restaurant was sued for not knowing what was in its food, and he and Patricia were sick of the casual way in which waiters dealt with their queries for more information. Even family trips on aeroplanes were stressful, as nuts were given out to passengers and Jaida's sensitivity was extreme.

As they looked deeper into the issue, John became aware of how widespread the problems created by food allergies were—sometimes with tragic outcomes. They followed the case of a young boy, Alex Baptist, who died in a Melbourne kindergarten in 2004 after most likely coming into contact with peanuts. In 2002 New South Wales teenager Hamidur Rahman had suffered the same fate. They were afraid for their daughter and unsure of what she could eat. The Ilhans felt alone and wanted more control over the situation.

One morning during their getaway to Daylesford, it suddenly dawned on John that there was something they could do about the situation. Why not try to educate people about nut allergies? Why not try to find a cure?

Giving back to the community was part of John's value system. It was the way he was raised and an important part of his religion. As much as he enjoyed spending money on the people closest to him — his family at Crazy John's and at home — he also loved supporting good causes in the community.

John was already a strong supporter of various charities; Patricia would often joke that if you caught John in the right mood he would give to just about any charity. He would also aggressively bid for items at charity auctions. At KOALA Foundation's annual Million Dollar Lunch in 2006 he bid successfully for a luxury holiday to Tuscany. At the time Patricia was pregnant with Aydin, and John, spurred on by the jovial taunts of 'Come on, she's finally given you a son, how about taking her to Tuscany' by the panel from *The Footy Show*, kept driving the auction item higher and higher. The price peaked at $40 000 before John closed out the bidding. In the end he was unable to take the trip, and gave it away as a staff award. A lucky Sydney manager won the luxurious holiday and took her mother.

There was a standing joke in the Crazy John's senior team that John should be kept away from all charities. He could not help but say 'Yes', genuinely wanting to help others. On one occasion a group of boys from a soccer club made an appointment with John to ask for help with sponsoring an overseas soccer trip. John was a huge soccer fan and so he listened patiently as the boys made their pitch. They needed money for the trip and also for their kit. At the end John asked them how much they wanted and they said $10 000. John replied, 'Why don't I give you $15 000 just to be on the safe side'. The boys were obviously ecstatic.

His enthusiasm sometimes ran away with him. In September 2004 John got into a spirited bidding war at a charity auction at St Catherine's School in Toorak, the school his daughters attended. The hotly contested item he was bidding for was a kindergarten painting by the kids themselves.

The silent auction escalated as John helped to push the bids up by $5000 at a time. The eventual winner paid a staggering $75 000 for the painting, saying he had bought it as an act of generosity on the anniversary of the September 11 terrorist attacks, but later admitted to some discomfort when he reflected on how much he had paid. John perhaps got the best deal because his daughters painted him a replica to make him feel better for missing out.

The story of John's involvement with the Shane Warne Foundation also illustrates how he was prepared to act spontaneously when he believed in a cause. 'I first met John via a telephone conversation', Shane recalls. 'I hadn't actually met him in person, but I wanted to approach him about supporting the establishment of the Shane Warne Foundation soon after year 2000. Feeling very awkward I rang him out of the blue after getting his number from former St Kilda Football Club President Rod Butters. John couldn't have been more welcoming and more delightful to talk to. He asked me what the foundation was for and why I wanted to start it. After I had explained why making a difference to children's lives was important to me, straightaway he said he'd help.

'I established the foundation with four other people, each putting in $50 000. Those people were James Packer, [Crown Casino founder] Lloyd Williams, [Sydney businessman] David Coe and John Ilhan. With that $250 000 we were able to set up the Shane Warne Foundation to the point that it has now given away a significant amount of money—$2.5 million—and has made a difference to over seventy-five different children's charities.

'After that we became good friends. His daughter Yasmin and my daughter Brooke attend the same school and became best friends, so we were always dropping kids off at each other's houses. We'd often talk about business and a bit about what was happening in his company and so forth, but we'd also talk a lot just as two fathers of girls who were growing up way too fast, and we would often get a chuckle out of that.

'John also gave a lot to different charities. I came to learn that about him. He didn't make a big deal about it; he just wanted to help. Sometimes the public never realises just how generous some people really are behind the scenes.'

For every public display of generosity there were plenty of other gestures John made that no-one ever knew about. He had no intention of telling anyone about them either, believing that true charity should not help the donator sleep at night, but simply help the benefactor. One day after John had passed away Ayse received a phone call from a doctor at a hospital in Turkey saying that John had put him through school and university so he could become a dermatologist. It was part of a fund that John had set up years earlier to help disadvantaged children in his country of birth receive an education, and Ayse's caller wanted her to know what John had done for him. In another instance, Ali and Nezaket encountered a distraught woman at the airport in Istanbul as they embarked on their return to Australia following John's death. She was upset at hearing the tragic news and told them that John had paid for all of her education.

John also personally supported the neo natal unit at Melbourne's Royal Children's Hospital (the hospital named many of the humidicribs after Crazy John's), the Salvation Army and many other organisations. He made many generous contributions that he did not even get a chance to tell Patricia about, and she only discovered them after his death, such as the $20 000 in funding he gave each year to the Brunswick Salvation Army so it could provide hot breakfasts for the local homeless. He had opened his first Crazy John's store in Brunswick and felt a particularly strong connection to that community.

John was acutely aware that his children would not grow up the same way he had. They would never go without and would experience the best life has to offer. As such, he was keen to ensure that his children would not grow up in a wealth bubble, but instead understand the social and economic hardships faced by many people in this country and around the world. 'I want my children to grow up as compassionate human beings that are not sheltered from the realities of life, but are instead inspired to make a difference to those less fortunate than themselves', John said.

He also made sure he showered his children with love and affection. All three girls remember how their dad would put on funny voices and tickle them, and the many pillow fights that would occasionally result in household items being knocked over and broken.

Jaida remembers how John would try to bounce them off the in-ground trampoline, their trips to the North Road Park and how he would coax her to breakfast. 'In the morning, he would rub his tummy and crawl over to my bed and slowly say, "Jaaaaaida, wake up!" and as soon as I got up he would run off saying, "Jaida wake up, Jaida wake up", because he was pretending to be really hungry and he didn't want to leave me upstairs so we could have breakfast together.'

The girls all remember how their parents would imitate each other. 'Whenever we'd call out to Mum, he'd say, "Yes, darling" [in a high-pitched voice] and he'd imitate her, and then if we said, "Stop that" to him, Mum would say, "What?"

[in a low-pitched voice]', says Yasmin. 'And sometimes when we'd call out for our mum, he'd say, "She's in my pocket" or "She's on the moon". Even though it was a bit frustrating at times, it was still funny.'

One of Yasmin's favourite memories of her father was their bike rides to Luna Park. 'I'd just gotten a new bike and we'd all go for bike rides to Luna Park', she says. 'One day he just took Hannah and I, and we were out for the whole day. I liked it when we went on bike rides. He'd also always go out to places to meet important people and then he'd come back and tell us about it, and I always felt it was really special because I was the only person who had a dad who got to do all those things.'

'Every night after dinner he used to get four blocks of chocolate and say, "I'm having chocolate", and we'd say, "You can't have any" and he'd keep eating it', says Hannah. 'Mum would say, "No, you can't have that!" and he'd say, "Just one?" and she'd say, "Nup, you're not having any".

'On the weekend he used to listen to U2 and have it up as loud as it would go. If there was a sentence he really wanted to hear, he would play it and rewind it back, and then play it again and rewind it back. It was so annoying! He loved U2.

'When he played games with us he used to tickle us. He used to grab us by the arms and tickle us, and then grab Jaida and tickle us. He would hold three arms at a time and then he used to just tickle you everywhere. That was really funny.'

At the Crazy John's head office in South Melbourne there is a wall covered in plaques of all the various charities the company has supported. John was happy with his philanthropic endeavours, but also felt that instead of just writing cheques he wanted to make a more lasting and focused approach to his community engagement. This desire for a change in his philanthropic philosophy came at the time when Jaida's illness was diagnosed. The Ilhan Food Allergy Foundation offered him the chance to make a significant difference in an area that was starved of funds for medical research, education and practical care.

Following the weekend in Daylesford, John set out to find the best allies with whom to establish the foundation. It was his characteristic business strategy—get the best people around you, give them the vision and drive, and the job will get done. Initially he sought out two of the most eminent scientific advisers—Dr David Hill, a pioneer in the field of food allergies having established the Allergy Clinic at the Royal Children's Hospital and internationally renowned for his research into milk allergies, and Professor Bob Williamson, who had previously run the Murdoch Children's Research Institute (one of Australia's leading research institutions) and is well connected in the Australian medical research community. During the 2003 Spring Racing Carnival Crazy John's showed its support for the Murdoch Institute at The Marquee on Crown Oaks Day by donating $50 000 towards the establishment of an international paediatric Magnetic Resonance Imaging (MRI) research centre.

From the start the Ilhan Food Allergy Foundation had very specific aims—research and education—opting not to try to replicate the substantial work in family support already being undertaken by groups such as Anaphylaxis Australia. The foundation's desire to keep its focus narrow, but drill deep, meant that it believed a large infusion of funds could quickly make a difference.

Its first task was to try to raise awareness of this growing problem. Australia has one of the highest rates of allergies in the world and a relatively high rate of peanut allergy sufferers—three per cent of Australian children are allergic to peanuts. At that time the number of Australians dealing with the risk of anaphylaxis on a daily basis was about 200 000.

A report compiled by Access Economics in 2007 found allergic disorders, including hayfever, asthma and others, cost Australia $7.8 billion per year in absenteeism from work and other effects. But the report added, 'This impact is likely to rise sharply, as the 4.1 million Australians currently affected—about one in five of the population—is expected to soar to one in four by 2050'. This translates to a massive seventy per cent increase in the number of Australians affected. The report also warns of increasing waiting lists in our hospital clinics and surgeries, and significant barriers to accessing specialist care in some regions of Australia.

For children the problem was also getting worse. The October 2007 issue of the Journal of Allergy and Clinical Immunology reported a five-and-a-half-times increase in the rate of Australian hospital admissions between 1994 and 2005 for food-related anaphylaxis in children under the age of five.

Schools were becoming aware of the problem as greater numbers of parents sought anaphylaxis action plans for their children, and education departments became aware that legally they might have an issue to deal with if they didn't act quickly, especially as allergy-related deaths in learning centres began to rise.

The Ilhan Food Allergy Foundation became busy quickly and in keeping with John's modus operandi on everything, it was decided the foundation should grab the public's attention. It produced a one-hour informational DVD on the subject of food allergies with the help of Channel Nine, which donated its studios for the filming and provided some of its stars to host the program. Producing this in just a few months was typical of John's style—a phone call to his friend and Channel Nine executive Eddie McGuire, and a studio and the stars were made available.

The foundation also wanted to offer practical help to families dealing with food allergies, creating an allergy-friendly cookbook full of recipes that exclude many of the major allergens, such as nuts, milk and eggs, called *Fast Ideas Safe Recipes for Kids*. It was initially sold in all Crazy John's stores, and then distributed to medical bookshops. The cookbook was given a high-end, contemporary look to help take away some of the medical stigma of dealing with food allergies. The foundation wanted to make a statement that it is natural to eat healthy and sensible food and no-one should be ashamed of their food allergies.

The biggest priority, however, in the words of John and Patricia in setting up the Ilhan Food Allergy Foundation, was to 'find a cure'. That meant looking for a vaccine so that the allergies that killed could have a front-line defence. The task of finding a vaccine meant medical research, and that doesn't come cheaply. John immediately said he would contribute $1 million towards this effort.

The foundation was fortunate that Melbourne—with its internationally respected medical research bodies such as the Murdoch Institute, Alfred Hospital and the Walter and Eliza Hall Institute—already had research into the area of food allergies underway, but it was only in embryonic form. What this research was lacking was funds, making John's call to arms to 'make a difference' all the more timely.

The Ilhan Food Allergy Foundation chose three different areas of research to support. The research selected was based on three cornerstones of the 'make a difference' mantra of the foundation—prevention, better understanding of the problem and a possible cure.

Perhaps the most immediately far-reaching of the research being financially underwritten by the Ilhan Food Allergy Foundation is taking place at the Alfred Hospital's Department of Allergy, Immunology and Respiratory Medicine. This research is investigating the 'induction of regulatory T-cell responses to inhibit "anaphylactic"-type immune responses to nut allergens'. What this means is the Holy Grail when it comes to food allergies—a vaccine to stop people dying from eating nuts. The foundation is looking at how to further support this world-class project, which will determine the potential for a safe and effective immunological therapy for people with nut allergies and assist in the development of better diagnostics.

In terms of prevention, the foundation is also supporting the Allergy and Immune Disorders Research Group Department of Allergy and Immunology at the Murdoch Children's Institute. The project being undertaken aims to investigate whether prenatal microbial supplementation—like Yakult—can prevent the development of food allergies and other allergy disorders. If this is proven, this treatment will have widespread application as a population-based preventive strategy against one of Australia's greatest health burdens. Such a strategy may have an enormous impact on the worldwide prevalence of all allergic disorders.

At the heart of the problem, however, is trying to understand why the incidence of food allergies is on the rise, both in Australia and internationally, especially for children. To this end the foundation decided to support a study of 5000 children—the largest in Australia—that tracks the environmental and genetic predisposition of children who develop nut, egg or sesame allergies in their first three years after birth. This research, taking place at the Murdoch

Children's Research Institute, aims to 'identify modifiable risk factors for peanut allergy in children'. This project will assist in determining environmental exposures that may alter the development, persistence and severity of peanut, egg and sesame allergy. Between 2007 and 2009 the Ilhan Food Allergy Foundation will have contributed almost $1.5 million towards the funding of these three key projects.

As the Ilhan Food Allergy Foundation has grown in prominence, it has developed a strong rapport with the state government, acting as an effective lobbyist in the area of food allergies. The foundation was able to work effectively with the then Victorian Health Minister Bronwyn Pike in 2007, resulting in the government announcing an extra $430 000 recurrent funding for the Food Allergy Clinic at the Royal Children's Hospital. This enabled more clinicians to see patients and slashed the waiting lists at the clinic.

The minister also established a working party—with the Ilhan Food Allergy Foundation as one of its principal members—to evaluate 'the best possible strategies that we can put in place to make sure that kids who have allergies are not put at risk', explained Minister Pike. That working party resulted in all Victorian schools being legally required to have active anaphylaxis management plans in place for any student who suffers from any form of allergy—a first for any state in Australia. Thousands of teachers have also been trained in the use of EpiPens, as well as other anaphylaxis survival and prevention techniques.

In 2008 Patricia was asked to speak at the prestigious national gathering of the Australasian Society of Clinical Immunology and Allergy conference and looked back on the foundation's achievements after just three years. 'I'm so proud of what we have been able to do in such a little period of time', she said. 'John would have been so proud that his position in life was to be able to give back in this way. Every day is still a journey to us when it comes to Jaida, but we are feeling much more secure about the future.'

It was not just the anaphylaxis community that John and Patricia had made an impact on. By this stage of the company's progression, Crazy John's was turning over millions, and various people and organisations hoping to gain support contacted John constantly. Of course, he couldn't say no.

Chapter 11

Getting the balance right

2006–2007

After almost fifteen years of relentless work, by 2006 things were starting to shift in John's life. He had made more money than he knew what to do with, was a father to four children and was moving away from the day-to-day operations of the company.

Crazy John's CEO Brendan Fleiter says that John never lost sight of the bigger picture. 'Commercially, he was quite comfortable with where the business was headed. The strategy that had been developed in 2004 and the mobile virtual network operator was on track, and in 2006 it was developing very well. The thing was, he had to contemplate whether there was life without Telstra, and the answer was yes.'

Barry Hamilton, Crazy John's Chairman, also remembers how changes within the business affected John. 'Because we were building the business, we didn't have sixteen stores anymore', he says. 'Once you get to 100 stores nationally, people had to be employed that John didn't know. It was a different business and John couldn't be as hands-on, and we had to put in place a management team that dealt with a lot of these things. During that time John probably felt that his importance within the business had diminished a bit and I used to say to him, "That's not right John, it's just different. You've got to give over some of that to people who are running the business in the state."

'He used to come in sometimes and say, "Well, what am I going to do today?" I was encouraging him to take on more of an elder statesman, diplomatic role outside of his company, and that's what he did. He was finding something to do. He was going out and talking to people—he was just so good at that.'

John decided to take Barry's advice, and in keeping with his passion for sport, discovered a much less physically draining game to soccer—golf. After picking up his first club in 2000, John quickly grew to love the game. He was a member of the Huntingdale Golf Club and had also started to play regularly with a group of people who shared his passion for and frustration with the game. They included Patricia's sisters' husbands Phil Eccles and Daniel Orlowski, Brendan Fleiter, Barry Hamilton, Nick Mitsios, Grocon boss Daniel Grollo, friend Mark Gibson, and real estate agency JP Dixon founder Jonathan Dixon and his colleague Peter Bennison.

Their time together on the fairways provided them with a good opportunity to unwind, have a chat and relax. 'We had a lot of fun together and golf was probably the thing that kept us enjoying each other's company as much as anything', recalls Barry. 'I certainly miss those times.'

There was one golf game where things did not quite go to plan, but John in typical fashion still managed to make a good impression. 'It was the first time he played at Sorrento Golf Club', says Barry. 'He hit the ball out to the side. We couldn't see where it had gone, and it had ended up on another fairway. We jokingly said to him, "Oh, I bet you've hit someone"—and actually he had. The fellow that he hit was a senior person in the club. He was a retired judge and a former captain of the club.

'We got back in [to the clubhouse] and someone said, "Did you know that a retired judge was hit out there today?" I said, "No", and went back and said, "John do you realise you hit a retired judge?" John said, "Oh, you're kidding". He was absolutely mortified that he'd hit someone. He said, "Who is he, where is he? I'm going to have to go and say something". I said, "Look, I don't think there was much in it. Don't worry too much about it. I'm sure if there was something in it we would have heard".

'Anyway, he wouldn't take no for answer, so he found this fellow and he put his arm around him and said, "Listen, I believe I hit you out there today", and the fellow said, "Yeah, I did get hit out there today", and John said, "I just want to tell you how sorry I am". And the fellow ended up smiling and laughing and saying, "Absolutely no problem, thanks for coming up, these things happen".

'You know, I don't think too many people would have done that, or could have done that actually. It wasn't a big deal, but John was really concerned that he had to go over and say something. That was the sort of people person that he was and he got the best out of people I think.'

Jonathan Dixon began playing golf with John in 2000. He has fond memories of their friendship, and was glad on one occasion that first impressions don't always last, because their first encounter was an argument. 'Johnny and I had the greatest fight of all time over the phone', Jonathan recalls. 'That's why they probably called him crazy. He was trying to buy a property and he was a real tough nut. Johnny and I had this huge battle and I said I think we'd better meet. But as soon as I met him, it all changed and we had a good laugh.'

Jonathan did sell him a property, in Bay Street, Brighton, before he sold him the luxurious home on Brighton's golden mile. Over time Jonathan helped him buy and sell many other properties. 'When we first started playing golf, John would aim in the opposite direction [of the fairway]', says Jonathan. 'He had the most unbelievable slice. But he must have had some lessons at some stage, unbeknown to all of us I'd say, because he could hit it straight down the middle in the end.'

Another of John's golfing mates, Peter Bennison, the Toorak director of JP Dixon, fondly recalls their times on the green. 'We used to enjoy our golf and each other's company, and we'd always have a good laugh', he says. 'John loved to laugh. He was pretty proud of his achievements, and he used to love the story where he started off. Jonathan and I aren't Broady boys, but we can mix it. We had a very similar philosophy on life and that's where we had our link.'

Their golf playing took them to many courses around Australia and internationally, notably trips to New Zealand and Tasmania. Although John was a teetotaller, he always enjoyed engaging in the various philosophical ramblings back in the club rooms, where nothing was off limits. He also enjoyed taking a walk after dinner of the first hole whenever they played at the Barnbougle Dunes course in Tasmania.

On another occasion in 2006 John invited Jonathan and his son, Todd, to Munich for the World Cup. 'I was in Italy with my family, and John said do you want to come to the World Cup? So I took Todd and we flew up to Munich. Here were my son and me—we were total ring-ins—and there was Lachlan Murdoch and all these absolute top guys. We're sitting there with John, and Graham Smorgon's wife turned around and [pointing to the other side of the stadium] said, "You know, you must be a very important boy, because my son's way over there!" We were right in the best seats, in the inner sanctum. Todd was having a chat with Lachlan, and I said to him, "Do you know who Lachlan is?" And he said, "Yeah, Lachlan". So that was just Johnny, he didn't care. If he wanted someone there and he could do it, he did it.'

Dinners with friends were also something John enjoyed, and he and Patricia spent a number of evenings with the former National Australia Bank Chief Executive Officer Ahmed Fahour, AFL Chief Executive Officer Andrew Demetriou, Daniel Grollo and their wives.

In an interview with the *Herald Sun* newspaper Ahmed discussed these evenings. 'We used to go out for dinners at least once a month with our wives', he said. 'It was the four wogs with our four Australian wives. The one thing we had in common, other than being first generation immigrants, was that we had a lot of care for this country and a lot of thankfulness for the opportunities we had been given. Because we'd all come out of the northern suburbs — Andrew out of Coburg, Daniel out of Thornbury, me out of Preston and John out of Broady — we all knew how lucky we were and how much we wanted to use our position to support harmony and do greater good.'[1]

According to Ahmed their heritage meant it was highly likely that their paths would cross, and that day came in 2005 when an NAB banker introduced Ahmed to John. What Ahmed did not know was that his brother, Moustafa, and John's late brother Gerald had known each other twenty years earlier.

Moustafa would later become John's trusted financial adviser and close friend, while John and Ahmed would work together as ambassadors for the northern suburbs, an initiative by the Premier, John Brumby. The two would also become business partners on a number of commercial arrangements.

John and Patricia also enjoyed evenings with their friends Seb and Sam Pir every couple of weeks, who by this stage had moved to Brighton and were closer to the Ilhans. Their dinners would always extend long into the night, and John, always one step ahead, would often ask for pen and paper at the dinner table to quickly jot down whatever idea had suddenly formed in his head. 'Uncle Johnny' and 'Aunty Trish' were like family to the Pirs. Their son, Taner, and Yasmin are one year apart, while Mikail and Jaida are the same age. Seb would give Patricia roses picked from his garden every time they visited, while John gave Seb a dog, Coco (named after Coco Chanel), for his birthday several years ago.

One of Seb's fondest memories of John was when Aydin was born, in January 2007. 'All through the night John had taken photos of the new baby son, and he took the camera from Trish and said, 'Seb, have a look at my prince. You see my son? I'm the king and he's the prince!' recalls Seb. The desire to have a boy actually came from Patricia, and when baby Aydin arrived, the Ilhans really possessed everything that they had ever wanted.

The happy occasion prompted a similar reaction by John when he met with another one of his friends, George Stefanou, his first boss from the old days at Ford. 'You couldn't have seen a person more proud', says George. 'I just couldn't believe it. He had seen the photographs that I have of my three [children] and he says, "Mate, you've got boys and girls" and you could tell by the tone of his voice that he was so proud. As much as he loved his daughters [a son] was just the icing on the cake. And I was obviously very happy for him. I said, "Mate, that's fantastic news".'

On another occasion, a week before John died, the Ilhans, the Pirs and a few others enjoyed a dinner at a Turkish restaurant. John ordered up a storm, as Sam recalls. 'It was funny because John liked to drink tea out of the little Turkish glasses. He said to the waitress, "Can we have tea in the little cups? But it's okay if you don't have them". She said she'd see [what she could do] and when she came back she served his in a little cup. John said, "This is just fantastic". All night he was cracking jokes about Seb arriving late for everything and always taking his time to eat his dinner. John was happy, cracking every joke possible. The teas were served all night and our table was so loud.' Sadly, it was the last time the families spent an evening together.

Ash Rady, his good friend and old colleague, always admired John's ability to balance and maintain friendships without money interfering. 'In his early days he was consumed by the business, and that's all he thought about. But as he grew older and he had a wife and kids he learnt that there had to be a balance in life, and he often advised me of that', says Ash. 'I was certainly someone who was an ambitious individual and I wanted to achieve good things for myself and my family, and work would consume me. I'd throw myself into what I had to do and he'd often pull me up and tell me there has to be balance in life. That was something I certainly learnt from John.'

For John, business was just a game. It was a way of supporting his family so that they could enjoy life, but it was also about creating employment and an exciting environment for those who worked at Crazy John's so that they could support their own families and enjoy life.

He was asked in an interview in 2005 whether the darker times were worth it. John replied, 'If I didn't have time with my family and see them growing up, or if I didn't have such a wonderful relationship, then perhaps I would think [it wasn't worth it], but I do and I never consider whether it was worth it. It's always worth it, not just because of what I have accumulated financially, but because of who I have become as a person. I am stronger and smarter, and I am always driven to achieve and see just how far I can push myself. It's not because I'm trying to prove anything, or maybe I am, but it doesn't feel like I'm trying to reach a certain place so I can be happy. I'm happy now and I'm just excited and curious about life and to see how much I can achieve in my lifetime. What difference can I make to the community, what legacy can I leave that I can be proud of?

'Sure I sell mobile phones, but I changed the industry and brought competitive prices to customers, and with the money I have accumulated I am now fortunate enough to be able to invest some of the spoils back into the community and make a real difference to people's lives. That's the only real benefit of having money. I love the lifestyle and I live very well, but that's only going to satisfy you on a certain level. Being able to really help will really make it all worthwhile.'

Another of John's loves was spending time in Portsea, and the Ilhans came to own a few properties in the exclusive enclave. An hour-and-a-half from Melbourne along the Mornington Peninsula, Portsea attracts the who's who of the Victorian A-list, with multimillion-dollar properties to match.

Patricia owns a house formerly owned by Margaret Porritt, the founder and designer of Feathers, a chain of boutique clothing stores. She and John bought it two years before he passed away. 'The house is absolutely stunning', says Patricia. 'It's eighty squares on an acre. It was on *Burke's Backyard* and has six bedrooms and six bathrooms, a tennis court, a swimming pool and is architect-designed. Margaret's son, David, is the architect who built it, and I don't plan on ever leaving.

'I bought the house without John ever seeing it. All he said was, "Can you just make sure there are two living areas so that the kids can be separate from us". This house is ideal for that because right up one end of the house are four bedrooms and a guest room and right down the other end is our bedroom. And opposite our bedroom is a massive, beautiful living room so it is like the adult part of the house, and then in the main part of the house are two other living rooms, so in fact it has three. I knew he would love it.

'But the front of the house is very understated, it just looks like a timber shed. It's one of those houses where you don't know where the front door is. So we get there and John said, "Oh my God, she's spent $4 million on a timber shed!" He almost collapsed at the front and I said, "No, it's okay. You need to pull yourself together because when you get inside it is stunning. You said you were going to trust me, so trust me".

'When you open the door you walk through an outdoor area, and then there's the front door. And when you open the front door there's this breathtaking home. Margaret said to me, "When you shut the front door behind you, you shut out the whole world". And that's exactly what this house is like. John needed the privacy. As soon as he walked in he said, "Oh my God, it's gorgeous", and he absolutely loved it. Every opportunity that we had to go down [to Portsea] we would go. In the end we had many wonderful times down there. It's a great house for kids.'

Also close to John's heart was exploring business opportunities in Turkey. He was being presented with offers from the

Turkish Government to invest in everything from the country's national telecommunications carrier—and possibly even opening up Crazy John's stores across Turkey—to bidding for the country's lottery licence.

Even bigger was a business mining proposal. At the time, a government bank owned the title to the mine that produces seventy-five per cent of the world's Borax, a natural mineral. Borax has a number of uses and is used all over the world, but Turkey didn't have a refinery and could only sell the mineral in its raw form. The government wanted to sell the mine and was looking for a new equity partner at a time when the commodity boom was just taking off.

Needless to say, it represented a monumental business opportunity to John. Moving into mining would have been a major extension of the Crazy John's business portfolio, as well as turning full circle and building part of his empire back in Turkey.

Apart from his business commitments in Australia, John had not completed his compulsory military service in Turkey and was reluctant to go in case he was forced to complete his national duty. In October 2007 he sent two of his close friends and business associates to Turkey—Billy Seri and Moustafa Fahour (the brother of John's close friend Ahmed Fahour, former CEO of NAB).

John and Moustafa had met through John's friendship with Ahmed Fahour. Both men shared a similar background and had built a solid friendship over the years, and John had met Ahmed's younger brother at one of the Ilhans' family gatherings.

Billy and John were old friends. Billy was eighteen when they first met and worked at a service station in Coburg, down the road from Mobileworld. Gerald and John would fill up their cars at the service station, and Billy and John clicked immediately. [Billy would later marry Sam Pir's sister, Dilek (Lou)]. John eventually became a shareholder in Billy's company, The Coffee Factory, as did Moustafa. John always loved to support his friends in their business enterprises, and even came up with the name for Billy's company. Billy is aiming to follow in John's footsteps by creating 'from zero to something' as he says. 'John was like the older brother that I always wanted', says Billy. 'He was like my idol, and I'll try to get to my goals like he did.'

The trip to Turkey came about in true John style. Billy and his wife, Lou, were at the Ilhans one evening when John suddenly stopped the conversation. 'John said, "I'm thinking of doing some stuff in Turkey". I said, "We've just had dinner, when did you think of that?" He said, "I just thought of it then". So we're listening, and he said, "I want you to go. Yes, I want you to go to Turkey". I said, "You're not serious. Are you serious? What am I going there for?" John said, "Just say yes or no". And I said, "Yes, I'll go". And it was just like that. So I rang Moustafa, as apparently I was going with him, and he just said okay, too. He was really big on people travelling and seeing the world. He would always encourage it', recalls Billy.

In the space of a week or so, John had set up appointments with business officials, Turkish business leaders and high government officials to discuss opportunities. John's connections with the Turkey community and all of the support he provided to the country meant that he had a great relationship with officials at the highest level.

The trip represented another instance in John's life that was more about giving back as opposed to making money. However, there were other aspects closer to home that required urgent attention.

Chapter 12

The hidden danger

2007

Maybe it was just tying up loose ends or perhaps it was premonition about his own fate, but at the start of 2007 John began putting his financial and personal affairs in order. John was not morbid, but he had once confided to Patricia that he did not think he would live to an old age.

In mid 2007 he had sold down his ownership in Crazy John's by 27.5 per cent to a combination of blue-chip investors, including the National Australia Bank, the Smorgon family and the Selpam Group (a long-standing Australian private company with a 100-year-plus history in property and business ventures). Prior to this John had been the 100 per cent shareholder and owner. He took great pride in three such prestigious companies wanting to invest in Crazy John's. John received about $75 million from the sell down and injected it straight back into the business.

By this stage John had started taking it slightly easier in his business life. He had the occasional day off mid week to play a round of golf and he was no longer working on weekends. The holiday house in Portsea had been renovated and John would often bundle the kids in the car on Saturday and head down to the beach house for the weekend.

Patricia believed John was tired of being in the public spotlight. 'The public pressure was taking its toll', she says. 'Everyone wanted a piece of him. There was talk about him becoming president of the Richmond Football Club. He would have done something like that if he wasn't working in the business, but he couldn't do everything.

'Look at Shane Warne—he can't go out for dinner anywhere. John was starting to become that way. People like to talk and say hello, and part of John really liked that. It's not really a bad thing, but we couldn't have a life back then.'

Brendan Fleiter, Chief Executive of Crazy John's, was convinced John was gently reassessing his priorities. 'He'd had fourteen or fifteen years of relentless work, his kids were growing up, the son Patricia and John had always wanted was born in January 2007, and he was moving away from the day-to-day operations. He travelled, he played golf and he wanted to spend more time with his family', he says.

Playing golf had certainly become one of John's biggest outlets to alleviate stress, and one of his most memorable golfing trips was a holiday to the United States with Daniel Grollo. The trip took place in April 2005 during the US Masters Tournament. For two very busy business leaders it was the longest holiday of their lives—they were away playing golf for a month. The pair would complete a round of golf in the morning and then proceed to Augusta National to watch the Masters live in the afternoon.

Daniel remembers it fondly. 'That trip was just a terrific time; John had such a great passion for golf', he says. 'I guess one of the reasons I connected with John was he was one of those people who was able to turn the tap on full at whatever he did. There were no half-measures. Golf was like that for him. Once he decided he wanted to play well, there was no holding him back. He wanted to play as often as possible to improve his game.

'When we played golf we didn't talk that much about business. I suppose that's because our respective businesses were so different—construction versus mobile phones. What we did sometimes talk about was how to overcome the hurdles put in front of you once you've obtained a high public profile.

'In some ways I was envious of John. He had a different way of dealing with his public profile than me. He could be more outgoing and say what he liked. That's because he didn't owe anyone anything, he was a completely self-made man. For that reason he had a great degree of freedom to frame his personality publicly.

'Sometimes he couldn't understand some of the things I did and the ways I did things, but then I was a third-generation business leader. I had a legacy to protect, I had a family name to uphold, which was the difference between us. For that reason I often thought he was lucky, and alternately he thought I was lucky.'

On the same trip John took another friend, Mark Gibson, who was with the two for six days. Mark remembers the various philosophical conversations about religion that took place, stemming from John's Muslim background, Daniel's Catholic heritage and Mark's own Atheist beliefs.

Mark was one of John's close golfing friends, and at the time, Mark was married to the Ilhans' close friend Beata Koropatwa. The four, as well as the children, would often holiday and have meals together, with Beata and John always laughing over silly jokes and their toothy smiles.

∽◦◦∾

For John it was clearly no longer about the money—he now had other drivers. He no longer felt any guilt about spending the money he had earned, as long as he gave back enough of it to charity.

After topping *BRW*'s Young Rich List for three years running, by 2006 John was past the cut-off date at the age of forty-one and he told the magazine that it was only the recognition he was after. 'I've always wanted to be the best in everything I do, because of that competitive background and having to fight for things. It's the same with the *BRW* Young Rich List. It's not the money that's the driver, it's just about being recognised.

'I think there's some subconscious, underlying guilt about having money. There shouldn't be because I've worked hard for it. But I think good societies will always look after the disadvantaged. Otherwise what's the point of it all? I just don't think everyone gets the same opportunities in life. How much money do you need to live on? How much bigger do you need your house to be?'[1]

He also had begun to analyse his strengths and weaknesses, and he wanted to let the next generation of entrepreneurs know that making mistakes was okay. 'I put a lot of value in making mistakes. The more mistakes I've made, the better businessperson I've become—mistakes are underrated', he told *BRW*. 'I know where to go, but I can't take [Crazy John's] there. I need the nuts-and-bolts people to help me get there. I'm more of a sales and marketing person. I'm not one on process, not one on scientific research, not an IT man and not a finance type. I know how to grow this business.' In fact, by 2007 John had named himself 'chief salesman' of Crazy John's. His trusted lieutenant Brendan Fleiter would run the Crazy John's business and John would look for ways to expand it.

Of course, John was always his own worst enemy when it came to trying to slow down. People kept coming to him with proposals he found hard to resist. One of the deals he was trying to get off the ground in 2007 was to become the owner of Melbourne's second soccer team in the newly formed A-League competition. Melbourne Victory had been launched and was performing well, and together with a group of other influential businessmen John tried to get a second licence to run a team out of Melbourne. The opportunity was just too attractive for John not to be interested. He'd played at the highest levels as a young man and now he had a chance to be the owner of a team in the national league in his hometown. Negotiations were still underway when John passed away, and then the deal collapsed.

Eddie McGuire recalls that John had spoken to him about his future plans. 'John had talked to me about possibly taking over the presidency of Richmond one day', he says. 'I had said it was up to him, but I did warn him about the time and energy it takes. I think if he'd lived he probably would have had a go at being president. I do think it would have been a great strain on him and I don't know how he would have handled the politics that surround footy clubs. I don't know how it would have all turned out. Having said that, John probably would have been successful at anything he put his hand towards achieving.

'He had talked to me about taking on Victoria's second soccer franchise in the A-League. I was never formally involved in the process, despite the *Herald Sun* writing a story that we were linked in this project. Once again I'd say if he'd lived he would have probably had a go at this. Soccer was in his blood.'

❦

In financial terms John was in a strong position. He had accumulated a lot of assets, and during 2007 he realised that his financial affairs needed more order. He had assets and income streams scattered everywhere. John had a diverse property portfolio that included everything from petrol stations, commercial properties, units and land with plans to build units, to an olive grove in northern Victoria. In fact, his property interests had grown to a level where they were worth almost as much as his stake in Crazy John's, and included the extensive prime real estate site in South Melbourne where Crazy John's had its head office. It was in the airspace above this site where he had planned to build the residential tower in the shape of a mobile phone. John knew that it would never receive approval and it never got the chance either, as Patricia sold the entire block after John's death.

John began working behind the scenes with his financial adviser, Moustafa Fahour. Moustafa was then working at Macquarie Bank looking after ultra-high-net-worth individuals globally and was almost fifteen years younger than John. He looked up to John as a mentor and the two had developed a very strong and trusted relationship.

Together they undertook a full financial check-up of John's affairs, separating which assets were linked to Crazy John's and which belonged to John and his family. This was important because when John passed away it was much easier to determine his financial legacy to his wife and children. 'When I first sat down with John I asked him where he wanted to be in five years', Moustafa recalls. 'That concept initially threw him. John lived for the moment; he had so much drive and energy. He was always throwing ideas around, building, growing, starting and acquiring new assets. However, for some reason he wanted to consolidate his financial situation and have a strong and sound financial plan. We determined his exact financial position and put everything in order, so that the size and composition of the family fortune was clear. If he hadn't conducted this and had left everything in a mess when he died, trying to unravel it all would have been very difficult.

'Through the development of a comprehensive financial plan we knew about every share, property dealings, philanthropic donations and the strategic direction on a lot of assets, and I worked with Patricia to help her understand this. There was something guiding John in 2007. If he hadn't done that work, Patricia would not have been as well looked after later on, especially given his entrepreneurial bent. It was impossible for Patricia to keep up with all the things John had on the go and look after the family at the same time. Was it fate or divine intervention? Planning ahead was certainly not in John's nature, yet he did all that hard work just months before he passed away.'

At the same time John began quietly taking more active steps to look after his health. He had not had a full check-up for two years, and no doubt driving his new health kick was the lingering doubt in John's mind about exactly what had happened to his brother Gerald and how he died at such a young age.

John had actually initiated his own private investigation into the circumstances surrounding Gerald's apparent suicide in early 1997. With the help of friends in the police force, he re-created the circumstances of how Gerald's body was found and interviewed neighbours about whether they had seen anyone else present the night he died.

The official police report suggested suicide, but for John there were some aspects that did not add up. Although the house was locked, Gerald normally kept the front door key inside the front door deadlock. Instead the key was found amid the grass in the backyard. Why would Gerald have thrown his own front door key into the backyard before taking his own life? There were also items of clothes allegedly missing, and surgical gloves were found at the scene. Was someone else present at Gerald's death?

'The circumstances around how Gerald died were always on John's mind', says Ayse. 'He genuinely didn't believe it was suicide. We all knew the coroner said that Gerald died of cardiac arrest, yet the police said it was suicide.' Whatever happened that night remains a mystery.

What John did not know was that by mid 2007 there was a hidden danger developing in his chest, and it was reaching a crisis point. John had developed ischaemic heart disease and coronary artery atherosclerosis. 'The three major arteries were completely blocked by cholesterol, which is an abnormal condition for a man with his lifestyle', says Patricia. '[Doctors] think it was the result of an enzyme in his liver that didn't function, which breaks down fat. We have that particular enzyme, but he didn't, so there was a constant accumulation. What your body and my body will do when those three major arteries become blocked is overcompensate by pumping blood through all the smaller ventricles surrounding the heart, but John's were very small. They were smaller than normal, so his body couldn't overcompensate. When the three arteries were blocked, there was nowhere else to go, so he couldn't get any blood to the heart. One was seventy per cent blocked, one was eighty per cent blocked and the other one was ninety to 100 per cent blocked. It was a time bomb, and it was also a very rapid onset of heart disease. He'd had a full medical check-up only two years before. No-one could have known that this would all develop so quickly.'

If John was becoming concerned that something hereditary might be influencing the health of the Ilhan men, he didn't show it. With the clock ticking on John's life, it was even more remarkable that he really began to shine by achieving so much outside the boardroom, as well as continuing to drive the Crazy John's brand. He threw more time into the Ilhan Food Allergy Foundation, which gave him a new lease of life on the public scene. This aspect of his public profile John seemed to enjoy, perhaps because he knew he was doing good.

In May 2006 there was an event at the Royal Children's Hospital in Melbourne when in front of then Victorian Health Minister Bronwyn Pike John announced he was committing $1 million towards the fight to find a cure for anaphylaxis. Every television station in Melbourne had turned up to the press conference and John just couldn't hide his enthusiasm. The minister had just announced a massive increase in funding to boost the capacity of the Allergy Clinic at the hospital. Waiting lists to the clinic would be slashed and there was momentum to try to fix the allergy situation. John's response was typically enthusiastic in front of the waiting media: 'We love you, Minister'.

He also began to believe he could make a difference in terms of better connecting the Australian Anglo-Saxon and Muslim communities. Around the end of 2006 and the start of 2007 suspicion towards the Muslim community was running high and the so-called war on terror was at its peak. John represented a successful moderate Muslim role model to counter the perception among some people that all Muslims were radicals.

John was proud to be invited by the Australia Day Council in Melbourne to make a major speech on Australia Day in January 2007. He had been appointed Bayside's Australia Day Ambassador, and took part in the citizenship ceremony and presentation of Australia Day community awards. John used the forum as an opportunity to promote better understanding towards the Muslim community.

The ceremony was held on a sunny morning in a marquee in the Kamesburgh Gardens on North Road in Brighton. The 250-strong crowd included the federal Liberal member for Goldstein, Andrew Robb, Bayside Mayor John Knight and prominent members of local Rotary Clubs, and it was covered by the local paper. During the ceremony sixty-five new Australian citizens took the national oath and John presented them with their certificate. After various speeches by the official speakers, he made the keynote address:

'For those present who will be becoming Australian citizens today, I have a special affinity with you. My parents came to this country from Turkey when I was just a few years of age and they, like you, embraced this country. Every day I thank my lucky stars that they made the decision to come to Australia.

'Australia has embraced my parents' vision that coming to this country rewards hard work. It truly is the land of opportunity. Australia has allowed me to begin and grow a successful business from very humble beginnings. I sometimes reflect back on my childhood in Broadmeadows and remember Jacana Primary, near Glenroy, as well as Broadmeadows High and recall the teachers who said I would amount to nothing. But then there were the people who believed in me and gave me support. I firmly believe behind every cheeky kid there is a natural born salesman like me ready to develop—it's just about being given a chance.

'What drove me more than anything was not letting down my parents, who had lent me $15 000 to start the business. They mortgaged their house to give me a start and I didn't want to let them down. There were nights when I was in my twenties still living at home that I would sit up wondering if my parents were going to lose the house they had worked so hard to buy because of me. That's an illustration of the family values that remain as strongly evident in a Turkish Muslim household in Broadmeadows as anywhere else in this great country.

'It's the same philosophy in a democracy like Australia— we all have the vote and we can influence our politicians. That means we all work together to make a better Australia, even in these more difficult times with the increased threat of terrorism. Let's not think that the model of multiculturalism doesn't work anymore. It is a great model for Australia and has served us well. My children and their children will always remember my origins in Turkey, but we will always be Australians first, second and third.'

John said later that it was the best speech he ever made because he believed his voice was now being heard across a range of issues. Suddenly other Muslims started coming forward about the same issue. Promoting his Turkish background was becoming more important to John as he got older, but at the same time he wanted to reiterate how important being an Australian was to him. He wrote an article for the *Sunday Herald Sun* on Anzac Day 2007 in which he talked about how a Turkish relative probably fought against the Australians at Gallipoli, but if international war were waged today he would fight for Australia.

John was also beginning to receive international recognition. He had always enjoyed a high profile in Turkey, but in 2007 the US Discovery Channel invited him to participate in a profile story that would be aired around the world. Being approached to do the interview was a coup. The series was called *Great Fortunes of the World* and only a dozen or so self-made millionaires had been chosen to participate. The producers had done their research in the US and Britain, but felt John's story was just too compelling to leave out. They dispatched a reporter from London, picked up a local crew and began filming.

This brought out the best in John. They took him back to outside his first store in Brunswick. He set up a trestle table on the street and with limited stock began selling phones again at the coal face—for the cameras of course. What the Discovery Channel did not anticipate was how recognisable John was. Soon a sizeable crowd had gathered, which wasn't bad for the middle of a Monday afternoon, and people started buying phones from him. He could rattle off the features of a particular phone even though he hadn't been a hands-on mobile phone salesman for over a decade. 'It's about knowing what the customers want. The customers are really your boss. They decide whether you succeed or fail', John told the reporter after he'd packed up the trestle table.

John also started to speak regularly to school groups. Growing up in Broadmeadows, one of the speeches he enjoyed most was when he was invited to address the year twelve graduating class of one of the most prestigious schools in Melbourne, Scotch College.

John used the speech to demystify the secrets of success—highlighting that any school kid was capable of achieving what he'd done. He told the young adults there were five simple steps to being successful in business:

'There is no single set of building blocks to success—it's different for each individual, but I will say there are some common themes to people like me who have created a massive business from scratch. These common themes are, firstly, family structure. When you start a business you work hard and to have family behind you is everything. It gives you the faith to keep going and an oasis if things don't always go right. My parents were my support structure in Broadmeadows when I started and now I have a wonderful family to go home to every night.

'Secondly, taking the leap. You can have all the best ideas in the world, but eventually you have to put your money where your mouth is. The best entrepreneurs never died wondering. Many of course do die poor, as only one in five small businesses survive in Australia, but you have to take the leap.

'Thirdly, toughing it out. There will be tough times. Managing cash flow for a new business is really hard. Those who keep fighting are generally the ones that stay in business.

'Fourthly, looking after the customer. Always remember why you are in business and who gave you the start. It is the customer, and if you forget about them and start thinking about the profits or the costs of servicing them rather than the outcomes, then the business will begin to die.

'Finally, staying true to yourself. If you start a successful business it is probably because you are doing something you are good at. As a business grows and the business owner has to delegate some responsibilities, it's easy for the original vision to get lost. The truth is that the owner or managing director drives the culture of the business and that should always be consistent.'

Ever motivated by the big picture, John had often spoken about exploring offshore opportunities and widening his horizons.

He had begun to focus on business opportunities overseas and one of his favourite places was London. John was even thinking—with Vodafone's help—of taking the Crazy John's brand to London. 'We'd talked about maybe going to live in London for a few years. Clearly John was headed for a change in his life as we began 2007', says Patricia. The Ilhans still have a house in the well-heeled neighbourhood of Belgravia, but his business plans for expanding into the UK were still in their infancy when John passed away.

John was also keen on getting Crazy John's into India. Due to high government taxation on mobile phones in India and a number of other factors, less than ten per cent of people in the country owned a mobile phone. Releasing the latest figures on the performance of the telecommunications sector in India during the first two months of the 2004 to 2005 financial year, the government said that connections were up from 2.595 million the year before to 2.874 million. That was a thirty-nine per cent increase, and John wanted a slice of this emerging, lucrative market.

Barry Hamilton said at the time, 'From my point of view India's probably the best next market for us to break into at this point in time. The European market is pretty well done and hard to break into. I don't think the Asian market lends itself to Crazy John's quite so well. India's English-speaking and has the English law systems and similar sports culture and a lot of people. Their middle class is huge—not in percentage terms but in actual numbers. They've got twice as many millionaires in India, for example, as we have people in Australia.'

In addition, it was widely known among the senior management of Crazy John's that John was looking to expand the company into New Zealand and open a chain of stores to test that market.

John's plan to explore opportunities in Turkey was another way in which he was turning full circle. And after setting off to Turkey on John's behalf in October 2007, Billy Seri and Moustafa Fahour were enjoying their business trip. Billy recalls, 'When we met with the Deputy Prime Minister in Ankara he gave us all of the options of what the government was selling. These included telecommunications, the tolls and Tattersalls—those guys were giving us all these options. We're thinking, "Oh my God". The government was looking at business in a different way, and trying to get more involved in partnerships with the world. They were so hospitable in looking after us because of who John was, of his reputation, and all doors were opened up to us. We were there for ten days and then we got the bad news.'

Chapter 13

The longest walk

2007

The morning of Tuesday 23 October 2007 dawned clear and crisp. It was the perfect morning for a walk along Brighton's bike paths, which run along some of Melbourne's best bayside beaches, with the sun glinting off the water. Spring was certainly in the air, and John Ilhan had a lot to look forward to that day.

Things had returned to normal in the Ilhan household with the end of the Muslim religious period of Ramadan, when John was not allowed to eat or drink during daylight hours, which was always a difficult period for those who lived and worked with him. Patricia and John finally had the son they had always wanted, with the birth of Aydin in January, and the older children were all settled at school. Holidays were being planned. John was going to take his eldest daughter, Yasmin, to the United States to see the popular Disney performer Hannah Montana in concert.

On that particular day John had a series of meetings planned. There was one scheduled for that morning with Patricia and the senior executive team of the Ilhan Food Allergy Foundation to finalise details of the menu for the foundation's first charity ball, the Rainbow Ball, to be held in November. It would ultimately turn out to be one of the biggest charity balls ever held in Melbourne, raising $2.4 million. John was excited about the ball. He had secured a Lamborghini, worth $500 000, to auction—and that was just for starters.

John also had a number of text messages to reply to that morning following a profile story on him that had appeared on Channel Seven's *Today Tonight* the night before. The show had been running a series of features on various high-profile Australians. Still to run was a profile story that Channel Nine's *Sixty Minutes* had recorded, but had not yet gone to air. It seemed that everyone wanted a piece of John Ilhan.

He was also riding high professionally. John had spent the past few months busy encouraging his store managers every night with text messages and phone calls to meet their sales targets, and finally it appeared his hard work was paying off. In addition, having switched over to Vodafone in 2006 as Crazy John's wholesale carrier, the company was notching up record monthly connections. That week he had also been up late talking to Billy Seri and Moustafa Fahour about the meetings they had been attending in Turkey.

With all of this swirling through his head, and perhaps to try to counter his hectic work schedule, John had started going for early morning walks. Walking had become his favourite form of exercise. This routine was a major lifestyle change for John because he was not a morning person, preferring to work late, sleep in and arrive at the office a little late in the morning. Although he had his own gym at home, he liked the walks because it meant he could get away from everyone, clear his mind and think about the day ahead. It was also very convenient—all he had to do was open the back gate in his beachside home and he would literally step onto the bike track or the beach.

As he ticked past the age of forty-two, John had decided to engage in more physical activity. Growing up he played sport, but the constraints of work and family had put an end to that, so now, like most men approaching middle age, he realised he needed to start exercising and shed a few kilograms. In his favour was the fact that, as a practising Muslim, he never drank alcohol. He had also completely quit smoking four months earlier. Prior to that he had cut back to one or two a day, but hadn't completely given it away. He did not carry a packet of cigarettes around with him, but his personal assistant, Amanda, was always on hand to offer him a few smokes if he asked.

So during his busiest year ever, John had got into the habit of putting on his tracksuit and runners, grabbing his wallet, a small bag and, of course, his mobile phone, and heading off for a brisk walk. There were always a few calls to make and a few text messages to fire off, but he also used the walk to think and not be interrupted by a ringing phone early in the day, something that was rare in his life at that point. Usually he would head out at about 6.30 am and return one or two hours later, often just in time to say goodbye to the children before they left for school. If they were out of bed, the children would watch him head off each morning—with him instructing them to start getting ready for the day and not watch television.

On that Tuesday morning he rose before Patricia, just after 6.00 am. Patricia's habit at that time with a young baby was to stay in bed until then ten-month-old Aydin awoke for his first feed of the day at about 7.00 am. As John had his morning coffee and prepared to get ready for his walk,

Yasmin, Hannah and Jaida drifted downstairs, switching on the television and talking about what they wanted to have for breakfast.

Hannah was feeling energetic. She declared that she wanted to accompany her dad on his walk. Initially John agreed, pleased to have some company. In many ways John and Hannah were alike. Both were natural sportspeople. Hannah's talents lie in gymnastics—she was in the Victorian Institute of Sport squad—but she is a natural at most sports, including tennis. Both were strong, driven and positive people, and they reacted to things in a very similar way. They clashed at times, but John always enjoyed spending time with her.

Just as they were about to leave John reconsidered. He couldn't promise to be back before Hannah would need to leave for school, so he told his daughter not to come. It was a twist of fate for which Patricia would be forever thankful. 'If Hannah had been with John when he died that memory would have stayed with her forever', she says. 'She has come to me and said, "Mum, what if I'd been there to save Dad?" When she's asked me that I've always said that no-one could have saved Dad, he died in an instant when his heart completely failed him.'

John left the house and began walking along the shared bike and walking path towards the city. He was heading towards Elwood Park. Football and soccer are played at the park on the weekends, but early on a midweek morning it is full of people exercising. John would often stop to chat to passers-by, and on this particular morning he chatted to three people.

Just after 7.00 am John entered Elwood Park and began to stride across the grass, but suddenly stopped and tumbled to the ground. A few people saw him fall, but did not react immediately. When he did not move, however, people responded quickly. Two people tried to revive John—they were part of a running group moving across the oval. A Brighton physiotherapist, Paul Visentini, and a student who had just completed a CPR course, Natalie Cape, began taking turns to give John CPR, once they had rung for an ambulance. Emergency services dispatched the nearest vehicle, which happened to be a fire engine.

A few weeks later Patricia visited the two good Samaritans who tried to save John's life to thank them for their efforts until the fire brigade arrived. 'They told me when they got to John he didn't have a pulse', recalls Patricia. 'When they watched him enter the oval, at first they thought he was doing exercises and had just collapsed, but then they didn't see him move. I went to see them because I wanted to know what happened in those final minutes. They didn't know who John was when they rushed to help, they didn't know he was Crazy John, they just acted out of kindness. I just wanted to chat with them to learn about John's final moments.

'The fire brigade and ambulance officers then stepped in and they worked on him for another thirty minutes. They worked on him for so long because John was so young. They hoped they could revive him. They did administer adrenalin to his heart, but it didn't have any effect. What the coroner's office has since said is they thought he died instantly because there was no blood in the heart when they performed the autopsy.'

Back at the Ilhan home the clock had ticked over to 8.25 am and Patricia had begun to wonder why John was not back. She got the three girls ready to take to school, but it was rare for John to miss saying goodbye. 'I wasn't that worried, but I thought it was unusual for him to be running late. However, I didn't think anything more of it. I just rang him to say I'm taking the kids to school and say see you later', Patricia recalls.

'When I rang John's phone a woman answered and I said hello and she said abruptly, "Who is this?" I said, "This is John's wife and by the way who is this?" She didn't answer that question, but instead asked where I lived, and then she identified herself as a police officer. I thought John had been mugged and someone had stolen his wallet and his phone. Then the policewoman said, "I'll ring you back in five minutes", and at that stage I started to get worried.

'I waited and time seemed to drag. Then I had a second thought about it and I decided to ring the policewoman back, but I couldn't remember which station she had said she was from. I first tried Albert Park police station, but couldn't find this policewoman. Finally I rang the South Melbourne police station and the same woman I'd spoken to earlier answered my call. Straightaway I asked, "Did I just speak to you five minutes ago?" and she said no, but I could have sworn it was the same woman. Then she said she couldn't talk to me right now and went to hang up the phone, but didn't hang it up correctly and I could hear a conversation going on in the background. Two people were talking and one was saying, "They tried to revive him but they just couldn't". I was listening to this conversation and saying to myself, "Come on, let's not jump to conclusions here". I kept listening and someone said, "One man tried to revive him for five minutes and then another took over".

'By that stage my heart had started to beat really fast, so I told my nanny to take the kids to school because I didn't know what was going on. Jaida was due at the Chinese practitioner as she'd hurt her neck on the trampoline and Ayse was going to take her, so she stayed home. The nanny just took Yasmin and Hannah to school. Baby Aydin was asleep.

'By then I was panicking and I tried to ring the number of the police station again on my mobile, but just as I did that my home phone rang and it was the New Street Medical Centre asking to speak to John. I told them he wasn't there and I was thinking, "I'd like to speak with him as well", and they asked that he call them back within two days, and I said fine.

'Immediately after that the doorbell rang, so I hung up the phone and went to the front door and I could see through our security camera that there were two police officers there. Even at that point, for some reason, it still hadn't dawned on me that John had passed away. I didn't know what to think. I thought they had come to tell me something important like he'd collapsed and was in hospital, and that I had to go with them urgently to the hospital.

'I let the police officers in my outside front gate and they were walking towards the front door and looking very serious, but they weren't rushing. That was strange — it didn't look like they wanted me to rush to the hospital. It was a policeman and policewoman and they were very nice. After I opened the front door the policeman said, "I'm afraid we have some really bad news for you".

'I became aware that the policewoman was standing close to me, I guess in case I collapsed. The policeman said, "As you know, your husband was out walking this morning and while he was out he collapsed. Two people saw it happen and went over to him. They realised he didn't have a pulse and they administered CPR, and I'm really sorry to tell you he could not be revived".

'While the policeman was telling me this he was looking down at his notepad, like he was checking off his notes, so that he got all his facts right. It was surreal. I said, "You're joking, aren't you?" I just couldn't believe it could be true. The policeman's response was, "I can assure you, madam, we would never joke about something like this".

'I didn't cry then; I was in complete shock. The police-woman was saying, "You need to sit down" and I was saying, "No, I don't". Then I said, "Please, let's backtrack a bit. What do you mean you couldn't revive him? You don't understand that you are talking about Crazy John. The whole community is going to be devastated, forget about me.

'I began repeating myself, "You don't understand what you are saying, this is Crazy John", and the policeman was looking at me as if to say he's still a man and he's just died. The look on his face said, "It's okay", but I kept saying, "This is going to shake up the whole of Melbourne — do you understand what you are telling me?" All he could say was, "I'm sorry".

'Then I asked what I should do. They suggested ringing someone and my first thought was there was no-one to ring. John's parents were overseas in Turkey on holiday. I said he had a sister, so the policewoman suggested ringing her, but I said I could go and see her because she only lives two doors down. First I said I needed to sort things out. Then I began to shake.

'At that stage I did sit down and I was just looking at the policewoman. There was silence for what seemed like a long time, but it must have just been a few minutes and she said, "Let's just wait". All of a sudden I went into this analytical phase and started thinking about all the things I'd have to do. All I could think about was, "I'm in charge of the family. The only thing that will really make me really sad is when I see the children, but I also have to tell his mum and dad and Ayse — John was like a second father to Ayse — and then I have to tell John's close friend Brendan Fleiter".'

Patricia asked the nanny to pick up her eldest two daughters from school. She didn't want them to find out the information from anyone else but her. While she waited for them to return she started ringing people, including Brendan, to tell them the news. She also rang her sister and her mother, and confided in her mother how concerned she was about getting through the tasks that confronted her. 'The first thing I asked my mum was, "How am I going to raise four children on my own?" Mum said, "Don't worry, I'll help you",' Patricia recalls.

Meanwhile, Jaida was watching television in another room, oblivious to all the commotion. 'The kids came back with the nanny and the nanny asked whether everything was okay, and I said no', recalls Patricia. 'The two older girls came to us and sat down, and I called Jaida in from the other room. I said, "Mummy's got something very serious to say to you, and you have to listen to everything I say. You know how Daddy went out for a walk this morning?"—by this stage Yasmin knew what was coming—"Well, Daddy was on his walk and he walked across an oval and he felt a bit sick and he collapsed on the ground. A lot of people tried to help him, but no matter what they did they couldn't get him to wake up".

'Yasmin said, "So he's dead?" and I said, "That's right, sweetie, you won't see him again". And then Yasmin completely broke down and started screaming. Hannah started crying, but I think it was only because she saw Yasmin crying. I don't think she realised exactly what had happened and that forever is forever. Jaida didn't cry, she was trying to understand what had happened.

'We were comforting Yasmin and that's when I got upset. Then I realised the only thing they had in life was me, and if I fell apart they would have no way of getting through this. All I kept saying was, "Everything is going to be okay" and "I'm going to get Ayse and bring her here and I promise everything is going to be all right".

'The next thing I told them was, "I want you to know that there will never be another man in this house. There is one father and that's it forever. It's about us now, it's about the four of us and we're a team and we are all going to stick together. Even though we were really close before, we really need to stick together because this is all we've got, so we really need each other".

'I sort of had them all huddled around me. We were sitting on the inside steps in front of the front door and that seemed to be a really good, calming moment, and all the girls reacted really well to that. I think they just thought nothing was going to happen to Mummy, so everything would be okay. Of course, deep down I was thinking, "Oh, shit", but in front of them I was saying it would be okay. The kids believing I had it together and we had a plan to move ahead together — that was the key to getting through those first days.'

Patricia then rang Ayse. After a few attempts the phone connected and she told her the news. She then went to Ayse's flat, which was only a few doors down the road, and Ayse began crying uncontrollably. 'Telling Ayse was one of the hardest things I had to do because she'd already lost one brother', Patricia says. When I told her she became so distressed. I kind of understood what it meant for her because she was the only one left of the children. All of our lives changed that day.'

Patricia asked Ayse to get some things together and come up to the main house. As they walked back to the house they ran into the same police officers who had broken the news earlier. They had returned with John's possessions — his wallet, bag and mobile phone. 'That was significant because then I realised there was no mistake', says Patricia. 'There was no going back.' They asked the officers not to leak the news as they wanted to let their family know first.

Ayse and Patricia then sat down and agreed that they would stick together. But Ayse had another phone call to make first. 'John's parents mainly still speak Turkish at home, so I knew it would be easier if Ayse rang them to tell them about John', says Patricia. 'When we came back to the house Ayse went into the kitchen and began trying to ring John's mum and dad in Turkey. I couldn't be in the same room when Ayse rang her parents.'

Ayse tried for some time to reach Ali and Nezaket. It was the middle of the night for them in Turkey. 'When Dad answered the phone I wanted to sound vague and break it to them easily in my calmest voice', Ayse says. 'I said softly, "Dad, I'm sorry I woke you. I just wanted to say that John went for a walk this morning". I wanted to let them figure it out themselves rather than blurting it out. "He mustn't have felt well. A couple of people tried to help him but it was like he was sleeping and he didn't wake up. Dad, we've lost him".

'Dad, with his calm belief that any form of anger or bitterness is an act against God, just said, "Kizim [my daughter], this is God's will. Stay strong. You know how strong we are. We've experienced a lot and we'll keep the family together. Don't leave Patricia's side and don't leave the children's sides". I could hear my mother crying in the background—she was just crying.'

The media quickly got hold of the story. The first calls from Channel Seven and radio station 3AW enquiring about a rumour that John had died came through to John's personal assistant, Amanda, at about 10.00 am. Someone had leaked the story. At that stage Amanda knew nothing of the truth and denied the story.

Now there was a rush to tell the Crazy John's staff before they found out through the media. Brendan Fleiter oversaw the writing of a media release, which was completed by 10.30 am. Part of the statement read:

> John did something very special in his life. He followed his dream and created a business that employed hundreds of people and provided real competition in the mobile phone business for the first time. He cared about looking after people.
>
> John's legacy will be felt forever in Australia because he offered something new to consumers through Crazy John's which will continue. He also established the Ilhan Food Allergy Foundation, which is dedicated to helping save and improve the lives of allergy sufferers everywhere.

Soon afterwards Brendan sent out an email to all staff at the Crazy John's headquarters in South Melbourne, calling them to an urgent meeting. He explained what had happened quietly, whereupon many staff members broke down crying, shocked at the tragic news. The media release was then sent out confirming that John had passed away that morning. Then the telephones really flew off the hook.

At 1.00 pm Brendan held a press conference at Crazy John's. He spoke to the gathering of about forty reporters—a media pack that was worthy of a major Prime Ministerial announcement. He spoke about John's pioneering legacy in the mobile phone industry and about it being unlikely to be repeated in Australia. Meanwhile, camera crews had arrived at Patricia's house in Brighton. By mid afternoon a sizeable crowd of supporters and well-wishers had gathered at the

Ilhan house, including Patricia's sisters, her mother and some of John's closest friends.

When Patricia did not answer the repeated requests for an interview at the front of the house, one media crew went around the back and put a camera over the fence to try to get some shots of Patricia and the children. All the curtains in the house had to be drawn in case the long-range lenses were brought out. If ever the family had thought that the world was closing in on them, now it really was.

After Ayse spoke to her parents it was then essential to get them home quickly. Under Islamic tradition John's body had to be buried within a few days. Organising the flight from Ankara via Istanbul to Singapore and then on to Melbourne proved to be difficult. The next few flights out on Turkish Airways were fully booked. Billy and Moustafa dropped all their other work and went to John's parents' house in Ankara, determined to find a way to get Ali and Nezaket home. Ironically, John had telephoned his two friends the night before to tell them that his parents would love to have them over the next day for breakfast. Sadly, their visit would be under very different circumstances.

Moustafa contacted his influential brother, Ahmed Fahour, who in turn asked then Qantas CEO Geoff Dixon for help. Qantas has a code-sharing arrangement with Turkish Airways and a few calls from Geoff Dixon saw the Ilhan party booked on one of the next flights as far as Singapore, where they transferred to a Qantas jet to Melbourne. If the normal commercial travel avenues had failed, Ahmed had approached his friend Jamie Packer, asking to borrow his private jet to bring back John's parents, which Jamie had agreed to.

'That flight was so hard, but John's parents were so strong', recalls Moustafa. 'We were all so focused on getting back in time for the funeral. I can tell you that John's death was big news in Turkey. We had to change flights in Istanbul and there were Turkish reporters waiting there for us. I don't know how they could have known we were flying at that time, but they asked John's parents a few questions and we kept moving. John's death was front-page news in Turkey. He was a hero there. His success made a lot of people in Turkey proud.'

Nezaket and Ali arrived back in Melbourne on Thursday morning, accompanied by Billy and Moustafa. They had been granted permission for a car to meet their plane on the tarmac, so that they could avoid customs and the media. John's parents were then driven to their Broadmeadows house, before heading to Patricia's house in Brighton. Both houses were full of people offering support, and boxes and boxes of food that had been delivered from friends.

By Thursday the family house in Brighton was full of well-wishers. Islamic tradition is that people go to support those who are bereaved, which helped get Patricia and the children through those difficult days. Patricia was entertaining scores of guests and slumping into bed at night exhausted, which meant she was seldom alone and had to contain her emotions. 'I just think you do what you've got to do', she says. 'You've got people coming to show their respects. Looking back on it, I surprised myself. I think when things are really bad I just get on with it. In fact, the worse the situation, the more I come out fighting. I think I've always been like that. I was like that during my teenage years, through my twenties and that was how it was when this happened.

'I do have my moments of sadness, but they are few and far between. I think my inner strength has always been there. I'd lost my best friend, my partner, the father of my children, but in the end I just accepted it. I believe there is a reason for everything. I have quite a strong faith.'

There were other things that had to be done in the days before the funeral. The *Herald Sun* and *The Age* newspapers in Melbourne had received dozens of tributes from friends of the Ilhans, but they had to wait until they had those from the immediate family before they could publish any. As a result, Patricia and Ayse had to find time to compose themselves on the Wednesday to write their own death notices. Patricia's note read:

> A loving and much loved husband and father. It is impossible to describe the loss of someone as beautiful as John. He was our inspiration and our rock.
>
> He loved his family more than anything. We always came first. We saw the man who cared so much about people.
>
> Our children will forever cherish the times they played with John and his dedication to them. Yasmin will remember how he could calm her when she was upset, Hannah will always remember how he inspired her to excel in sport, Jaida will remember the kisses and tickles, and Aydin will remember the song he used to sing to him.
>
> I will remember that we were true soul mates. He always knew what I was thinking.
>
> John cared so deeply about the people he worked with, his friends and business colleagues and the charities he supported.
>
> We have been overwhelmed with the messages of support and love we have received. We thank you. John inspired us all so much with his passion and he will continue to do so. He will be in our thoughts and hearts forever. Love you always,
>
> Patricia, Yasmin, Hannah, Jaida and Aydin.

Ayse's notice was published next to Patricia's:

> My Loving Brother. John was my everything, my brother and the inspiration who guided me through life and filled me with strength.
>
> John showed me love, compassion and generosity. A helping hand whenever I needed him.
>
> I saw the difference he made to the lives of everyone he touched. He was a true leader.
>
> I will cherish wonderful memories of his love for his family, our Mum and Dad, our brother and his friends and colleagues.
>
> John was the man I admired and the brother I adored. The man that taught me my whole life that there are no problems just obstacles and we just need to find ways around them.
>
> John, you will always be with me with your whispers of guidance.
>
> Love always, Ayse.

Hundreds of tributes were published. Staff from Crazy John's wrote their own public notice, part of which read:

> John can never be replaced, but his legacy will live on. The staff at Crazy John's are more determined than ever to carry on John's vision. That's the way he would have wanted it. Expect to see more of the innovation and great deals that have set Crazy John's apart from any other mobile phone retailer. The values of focusing on customer service are deeply embedded in the company thanks to John.

Everyone associated with Crazy John's sends on their
deepest sympathies to John's wife Patricia and his children
Yasmin, Hannah, Jaida and Aydin.

John will always stay in our hearts.

Patricia and the children also had to be educated in the way
of a traditional Islamic funeral, which was scheduled for
the Friday morning at the Broadmeadows Mosque, in King
Street, Broadmeadows. Ayse explained to the girls what
would happen and warned them that they would see their
father one more time.

Patricia admits that much of the day of the funeral was a
blur. Her parents and sisters arrived at her house so they could
all travel together to the mosque. They arrived at 11.00 am and
Patricia and the three girls were ushered into a little chapel.
Aydin was at home with a babysitter.

An important part of the Islamic ceremony is the family
viewing of the body just prior to the funeral service. 'The
worst thing about that event was that John's dad said to the
kids, "Just kiss him goodbye",' Patricia recalls. 'His dad didn't
mean any harm by that, he thought it was natural, but I was
dead against it and I stopped them immediately, and John's
dad got a little upset. But I explained to him later that I didn't
want them to feel how cold he was. I mean, he had been
in a freezer and I didn't want the children to know that. In
fact, when I went to the coroner's office and kissed him, that
was the biggest shock for me—how cold he was. I think
that decision, for the kids not to kiss their dad, helped shield
them, because I didn't want to address those questions from
the girls about why he was so cold. So if you ask the children
now about their last vision of their dad, they will just say he
was asleep. We then moved into an adjoining room and the

Turkish ambassador's wife was there. We waited for about fifteen minutes until the service started.'

They moved into the main area of the mosque for the service, joining the other hundreds of mourners inside and the crowd standing guard outside. Lasting about forty minutes, the service was entirely in Arabic and comprised various prayers about protecting the soul. Ayse explains, 'The prayers are about making that transition as smooth as possible, so that the angels will look favourably upon him as they take him to the next world.'

From there, the coffin was placed in the hearse and Patricia and the children got in the car behind. A huge convoy of cars followed, all driving out to Fawkner Cemetery for the burial. Traffic wardens were needed to direct the cars more than one kilometre from the cemetery entrance.

The Ilhan family plot is decorated with white roses, which were planted on top of three adjoining graves. When Gerald passed away, Ali and Nezaket reserved two plots next to Gerald's grave for themselves. John is now buried in the middle grave, with the site on the right reserved for Nezaket. Ali felt that a mother should always be there with her children. The two men's graves are topped with black marble.

Muslim tradition requires the body to be prepared in a particular way, and Patricia had asked Billy Seri to ensure John's coffin and every detail of the process was handled correctly. A great honour was to carry the coffin, and the six pallbearers included Ali, Billy and Seb Pir. Another Muslim tradition is the symbolic gesture of throwing dirt into the gravesite after the coffin is lowered, and there were many people who wanted to pay their respects. There were more prayers said at the burial before Ali and Nezaket hosted more than 200 people at their house after the proceedings.

∽∘∿

Patricia's one comfort is that when John died he did not suffer—it was all too quick. 'Looking back on what I know now, poor John didn't have a chance. He was a walking time bomb. There was no bringing him back and there was no possibility of survival once he had a heart attack—three arteries were completely blocked and unless there is blood in the heart you can't start it. John had developed severe heart disease. He'd had a full medical check up two years earlier and there was no sign. He couldn't have known what was going to happen to him.

'The call I got from the medical clinic the morning John died was remarkable for its timing. It was the outcome of some blood tests he had finally had done. His doctor had been onto him for some time to get them done, and I'd been looking at the referrals for six months. That drove me mad. He'd always be too busy to go or he forgot to fast ahead of the tests. Finally, he went to get the tests done, for cholesterol and a few other things, the Wednesday before he died. It was on that fateful Tuesday that we got the cholesterol results. It was 7.5, which is high, but not deadly high. The clinic was asking him to come in for more tests.

'What has stuck with me is he got the referral for those tests six months earlier. He kept saying that he would get them done and I just looked at the referral on our bathroom shelf for months. I'd had so many arguments with him to try to get them done that he got sick of my nagging. Maybe if he'd just had those tests done earlier they would have led to other tests and the problem would have been revealed. That's the really sad thing.'

Chapter 14

Turning full circle

2007–2009

The days after John's death and the funeral service were long and blurred for the Ilhans, and both the Brighton and Broadmeadows homes were constantly full of well-wishers, there to provide support and share the family's grief. Ali and Nezaket had now lost four sons, while Patricia had lost her soul mate and the father of her children.

Patricia's closest friends rallied around and supported her with the practicalities of hosting various guests over the first few weeks. The Ilhans' small but fiercely loyal friendship group was like family, and now they were all there when Patricia needed them. The news had hit the Ilhans' good friend Seb Pir especially hard, and he had wanted to bury his best friend, and to 'make him comfortable' at the funeral. He still visits John's gravesite with his children to have a chat.

Sam Pir comments, 'Patricia is just a beautiful person. She always stood behind John and allowed him to do whatever he wanted, because he worked so hard. When he died I said to her, "Now you're the father and the mother, so you can stand wherever you like".'

There was a long list of issues for Patricia to confront and little time for her to think about herself. In many respects Patricia had to learn how to deal with everything largely by herself and just move forward step by step, but quickly. John had spoken to Patricia about donating his organs several years earlier, expressing a desire to donate whatever could be used of his body. She wanted to honour his wishes. 'I knew John would have wanted every organ possible to be donated, however, it was already forty-eight hours by that stage and they could only take his brain and cochlea. So he actually had no brain when he was buried. He wore a very high shirt so you couldn't see the incision marks', she says.

The donations were arranged through the coroner's office and Patricia was presented with two plaques—for Mustafa Ilhan and John Ilhan. She was also given a 'tree of life' with branches of gold leaves representing how John's contributions have affected others' lives. 'They continuously remind me of what he gave them, and I'm so pleased I did it', Patricia says.

'I've never lost anyone in my family before, so I've never had to grieve for anyone, thank God. I think you need to grieve in private and I just learned that about myself', Patricia comments. 'I felt all the commotion in the house after John died, with scores of people visiting. It was good because it taught me to not grieve openly and I think my friends felt they didn't want to leave me by myself. So often in those early days I would get to bed so tired and exhausted that I didn't have the energy to lose it. I would fall asleep straightaway.

'Weeks passed and finally people stopped coming to the house, and I had that moment to myself, but by then I'd had time to speak to my family and friends and put things into some sort of perspective. For that reason I never really experienced that dreadful damaging grief that other people suffer. I sort of missed it and I've been waiting for it to happen, but it hasn't.

'The amazing thing is I don't worry that it might hit me one day. I feel more and more confident about the future and my ability to raise the children. That's certainly a big difference from the immediate days after John passed away, because my biggest concern was how was I going to raise four children on my own. If I was ever going to have a moment where I wasn't going to cope with John's passing and the incredible task ahead of me, it would have been back when John first died, but it didn't happen. Today, the future doesn't seem like such an incredible task as it did back then.'

Patricia takes comfort from the events that occurred prior to and following John's death, in 2007 and 2008, such as John getting his finances in order and the fortuitous sale of Crazy John's. They suggest to her that perhaps larger forces were at play. Whatever drove these interconnected events, she is thankful for it.

'In those quiet moments, I really believe many things have happened to assist me and the kids', Patricia says. 'I don't know whether people believe in coincidences, but a lot of things have happened to me that I couldn't explain. For example, the way John passed away. He said goodbye to the kids that morning, gave them a kiss and he died in a park. I've had so many letters from wives whose husbands have passed away the same way as John, but who had a cardiac arrest at home and died in front of the kids. Instead, John died in a really nice place. I often think about it; he could have been holding the baby. The doctor says he died instantly and he wouldn't have known what hit him. If that had happened, he would have dropped Aydin.

'The way he died is remarkable. He went for a walk along the beach and met three people he knew, and then just fell asleep in the middle of a soccer oval—and soccer was his great love. Another thing on the financial side is three to six months before he died he changed everything so all the assets were in my name and he ensured that the kids and I were completely financially secure. His financial advisers cannot believe he did that work just three months before he passed away.

'If he had passed away earlier, I would never have got my boy Aydin. I was the one who wanted to have a boy. Why do I get him and then ten months later I lose John? Was what happened all about looking after me? I pray for a boy for ten years and get Aydin, and then immediately I'm confronted by this strange twist of fate. All these questions don't worry me, in fact it's all a comfort to me.

'Dealing with John's passing, I draw a lot of strength from the children. One of them sleeps with me every night; they take it in turns. So I'm never in bed alone, and that totally fulfils me because I've got a big bed and there's nothing like a cuddle from the kids. I always know they are there.'

Patricia and John's close friend Beata Koroptwa was a constant source of support during those times, and she and her husband at the time, Mark, made a promise to help raise the children. 'Aunty Beata' helped look after the children when John died, but also took on an authoritative role in protecting Patricia. It was not until a few months after John had died that the two could talk about his passing.

'Patricia and I were very close, but our friendship just took on a new dimension', Beata comments. 'By Christmas time, we sat together at the Sorrento pub for five hours and we were able to bring out, as I call it, that compartment. There was no-one around and they actually had to ask us to leave because it was so late, but … we were able to actually talk about it, what had happened that day and afterwards.'

When the activity at the house subsided, Patricia's main focus turned to her children. She was worried that there could be an underlying hereditary medical condition. She was monitoring how the children were dealing with the loss psychologically, and she had to move swiftly to protect and secure the wealth that her husband had left them.

The first thing Patricia needed to do was to get to the bottom of what had happened to John. The day after his death Patricia gave the coroner permission to perform a full autopsy on John. When she received the coroner's report she asked her general practitioner to explain it in layman's terms. In effect, his coronary disease had blocked his arteries, and the unusually small veins that supplied blood to John's heart were unable to compensate for the problem.

As a result of what the autopsy found, Gerald's autopsy was re-examined by the coroner and the problem was discovered to be a hereditary condition. The children and other family members needed to be checked as soon as possible. Ayse was checked first and received the all-clear, so the theory then was that the problem might be passed on only to the males of the Ilhan family. Two people then became the focus of the investigation—John's father Ali and his son Aydin.

Ali underwent a number of tests, one of which, a stress test, showed that his heart did not have a normal rhythm. He then had an angiogram and a CT scan, which revealed that Ali had the same medical issue John and Gerald had, and a heart bypass operation was ordered. It was also discovered that he had one less artery compared with most people.

It generally takes about forty-two years for the concentration of calcium in the body to build up sufficiently to block the arteries in the heart, and most people by the time they are thirty-five should have had a heart check. Remarkably, it was the older man, who had worked incredibly hard all of his life, who managed to cheat death. In early 2008, Ali had the heart bypass operation—an operation that his doctors said would add an extra ten years to his life.

The children's tests had to be completed in stages. There were MRIs and stress tests and others that had to be completed, and Patricia only got the final all-clear in mid 2008. However, the specialists suggested Aydin be tested every two years for the rest of his life as a precaution. 'If the problem arises in Aydin we can stop it', says Patricia. 'Now we know there is a hereditary problem we can plan ahead for it.'

On the business front, in the weeks that followed John's death Patricia was forced to be more actively involved in the day-to-day running of Crazy John's. Brendan Fleiter became Chief Executive, but as controlling stakeholder in the company there was a daily stream of couriers to Patricia's house bringing documents for her to sign and there were constant phone calls. There was also a weekly marketing or product development meeting and a monthly board meeting. This process began in late 2007, just a month after John passed away, and continued through most of 2008.

For Patricia, juggling family, the Ilhan Food Allergy Foundation and the business was beginning to take its toll. 'The kids were asking all the time why I was never there', she recalls. 'I mean, they had a lot of support, and Ayse was living with us, but I'd be dropping them off at school and then going to a series of meetings. I also realised that I had so much of the family's wealth tied up in the business, but I ultimately didn't have any control over what was going on. I probably should have set up an office at Crazy John's and looked over things. That's what John was able to do when he was alive and worked full time, but I wasn't.'

The pressure continued to build, so Patricia decided to test the waters and find out what Crazy John's was actually worth. It came about during the process of looking into and selling off a range of John's other assets, such as an olive grove he owned near Shepparton. In total there were thirteen major property assets that needed to be sold, and Patricia, with the help of Moustafa Fahour, managed to sell everything off before the economic boom turned to bust.

'In early 2008 I had a merchant bank value what Crazy John's was worth, and I was surprised by the findings', Patricia comments. 'From then on I had it in my mind that I really only wanted one buyer for the company—Vodafone. Vodafone was already Crazy John's reseller, following the end of the Telstra deal. They understood the business and could clearly see the potential. They were also what Crazy John's needed—a global company with major expertise and a strong balance sheet.

'I'd been putting funds into Crazy John's after John's death, because every new product development or systems upgrade needed more investment. I didn't regret investing that money, but by the same token the investment needed in the longer term required Crazy John's to have a major partner.

'There was also one thing that comforted me when I began negotiations to sell Crazy John's and that was the various conversations I had had with John [about selling the business] before he died. I remember saying to him, "Why do you need to keep working fifteen-hour days? It's time to slow down".'

Patricia, with the help of Barry Hamilton and Brendan Fleiter, began negotiations with Vodafone to sell Patricia's stake in the company, which stood at close to seventy per cent. The official negotiations began in July 2008 and only took around two months, which was fortunate because the global financial crisis was about to hit Australia. The deal was done just weeks before the demise of US investment bank Lehman Brothers on 15 September 2008, which sent shockwaves through the global financial system and resulted in investment budgets around the world being frozen.

In many respects the sale to Vodafone was not unexpected. When John had signed a deal with the company twelve months earlier for it to become Crazy John's official carrier, a clause was inserted allowing Vodafone first right of refusal to buy the company outright. The offer to buy also came at a time when Vodafone was aggressively chasing market share, and for Vodafone Australia's chief executive, Russell Hewitt, it was a purchase that would have barely raised an eyebrow at the company's head office in London, which was used to dealing with acquisitions ten times that size. In addition, Vodafone's emerging markets boss, Paul Donovan, had once been second in command at Optus and understood the value of the Crazy John's business in Australia.

Russell Hewitt released a statement when the deal was announced on 5 September 2008, praising the Crazy John's technology platform for billing and customer service. 'These days, well-oiled, flexible platforms that scale well—that is, cope with fast-growing customer numbers without crashing—provide both cost savings and competitive advantage in matters such as being quick to market with new products.'

Vodafone was also similar to Crazy John's in other ways, with its more than 120 stores, and the company represented a way to grab significant additional retail reach to try to take on the might of Telstra in the Australian marketplace. The Crazy John's brand was a good fit with Vodafone — its offers of 'value for money' and the 'best deal' are only slightly different from Vodafone's emphasis on technology, style and mobile content. Vodafone could use the Crazy John's brand to test new customer offers or bundle deals that could be migrated across the whole Vodafone network, if successful.

The final price for Crazy John's was agreed to and the final negotiations were completed while Russell Hewitt was in Beijing for the Olympics in August 2008. 'I remember we were trying to get hold of Russell to complete the deal', says Patricia. 'It was one day when we were having a board meeting, but he was climbing the Great Wall of China. He also didn't have very good mobile reception. So we were in the board meeting and Russell was on speakerphone, yelling down his phone from the Great Wall. It was quite a surreal moment.

'Some things are meant to be. If we hadn't got a sale then, in just a month's time I doubt that Vodafone would have continued negotiations. The financial crisis was growing and everyone was battening down the hatches. Once again it was fate looking after us. That sale has set up my family for life — and hopefully my children's children as well.

'The hardest part about selling out was trying to explain the decision to those staff members who had been so loyal, some of whom had worked at Crazy John's since the start of the business. It wasn't that I didn't believe in Crazy John's anymore, it was just that it was going to be too hard to both run my family and the business. Maybe if Aydin was older I could have stepped up my working hours, but the reality was he was only two in 2008 and I needed to be with him.

'Before the sale was announced publicly, I had the most trusted staff members who John had employed come over to my house and with Ayse I told them first. I didn't want there to be any surprises. I needed to face them and explain why I was selling out. I wanted to part with Crazy John's in the right way. I'm prevented from revealing the sale price to Vodafone of my controlling stake in Crazy John's, but I can tell you that the price was so good I believe even John would have said yes to selling the business. The time was just right.'

Another legacy of John's that will endure is the Ilhan Food Allergy Foundation. In the wake of his death the foundation received a mass influx of donations, and with Patricia's involvement remains just as active today in supporting research to find a cure for anaphylaxis.

The foundation held its first Rainbow Ball in November 2007, which turned out to be one of the biggest fundraising events ever held at Crown Casino. It was attended by various high-profile personalities, and included performances by singer Vanessa Amorosi and food by Tobie Puttock of Fifteen Melbourne. The funds raised allowed the foundation to ramp up its financial investment into medical research. In 2008 and 2009 it invested close to $500 000, which resulted in the foundation being able to fast-track what could be the world's first nut vaccine.

'We are really proud of what John and Patricia have been able to achieve with the foundation', says Ayse. 'I think one of John's biggest legacies might be that he helps save hundreds of lives of children who might have died due to food allergies. Before John and Patricia came along food allergies didn't really have a major profile. But they helped personalise the issue and John managed to promote it, so everyone heard about it.'

Another successful fundraising event held by the foundation is the annual John Ilhan Tribute Lunch, held in conjunction with the Rotary Club of Brighton, of which John was a strong supporter. The second lunch was held in July 2009 with Eddie McGuire as guest speaker and a panel made up of past and current AFL presidents on hand to help auction fundraising items.

At the end of 2007 John's golfing friends decided to make a permanent gesture to John and his family. They approached the Bayside Council for approval to erect a park bench with an engraved plaque on John's favourite stretch of Brighton Beach. Only people who have made a significant contribution to Brighton can be honoured with their own bench, and as befitting John's reputation, his is at the front of the park closest to the beach. It is also just a few hundred yards from the front door of his house.

In a special ceremony Jonathan Dixon, Peter Bennison and Barry Hamilton presented the plaque to Patricia along with a bunch of roses. The inscription reads: 'In fond memory of John Ilhan. Loving husband of Patricia, devoted father to Yasmin, Hannah, Jaida and Aydin. A great friend to all his golfing mates. We miss his laughter 1965–2007'.

Closer to John's old home in Broadmeadows is another annual event—the John Ilhan Cup soccer competition. The matches are held at the Broadmeadows Valley Park Reserve, which was renamed the John Ilhan Memorial Reserve in 2008. John's passion for soccer and the lack of sporting facilities in his former neighbourhood prompted him to lobby the state government for funds to develop the soccer reserve.

At the time the Premier, John Brumby, and the Hume City Council pledged to contribute $250000 each to build a synthetic soccer pitch, which would provide the community with a reserve of Victorian Premier League standards. 'He was a great philanthropist, giving an enormous amount of his wealth back to the community through a great number of charities', commented Mr Brumby. 'Mr Ilhan was also a great promoter of Victoria and, in particular, Melbourne's north-western suburbs, and it is fitting that this recreation reserve, which is used by so many young people and families every day, is named in his honour.' Ultimately, it would enable future generations of soccer players from the area to play socially and competitively. The reserve is now home to the Hume Football Club.

It was at a memorial service on 12 November 2007 that many of the people whose lives John had touched had the opportunity to publicly remember him. The service was held at the John Batman Theatre at the Melbourne Exhibition & Convention Centre and was attended by about 1000 people. The event was hosted by Eddie McGuire, and speakers included John Brumby, Ahmed Fahour and Ash Rady. In a touching tribute about 100 Crazy John's staff walked on stage during the service, lit candles and placed them on a steel frame. When fully illuminated, the frame revealed the initials 'CJ'.

Now without Crazy John's the Ilhan family has turned full circle and Patricia says she has learned a great deal about her husband since he passed away. 'I've met so many people who said John sold them their first phone', she says. 'Maybe John sold more phones in the early days than he let on. I've also met lots of people who benefited from John's random acts of kindness—helping out the son or daughter of someone who had approached him [for assistance] or buying an airline ticket for one of his staff whose parent had passed away in Europe so they could go to the funeral. John influenced so many people. The more I learn about the good things John had done in the business and the community, it all helps to consolidate this view I have about fate and destiny and what was meant to be.'

What was vital to John was passing on his legacy to his children—ensuring that, although they would grow up privileged, they understood the value of money. 'Desire is a very interesting thing', John told *BRW* in an interview in 2006. 'How does one get desire? I believe your environment makes you what you are. Because nothing was given to me, because I fight for everything, because I had very little, everything I achieved was so sensational. That's what I am trying to teach my kids because they have everything. I want to make them understand the value of money. They will not work in this business as long as I am alive—I don't think it's fair to set those expectations. They would never feel that they are their own person.'[1]

Interestingly, John also told *BRW* he never wanted to retire—although he did not say that he wanted to stay with Crazy John's forever. 'Retiring means giving up on life', he said. 'You've got to do something—work at a hospital, work at a football club. I'll always do something. If you are working, you are stimulating your brain.'

In another interview John pondered whether he would ever lose the fire in his belly to stay on at Crazy John's. Patricia wanted him to go into politics with his strong sense of community and justice, but she concedes sport may have been John's next major direction. She believes it is likely that in time he would have run for president of his beloved Richmond Football Club.

Many of John's friends and colleagues are gratified in one way that he went out on top. 'He was liked and admired by many people', comments Brendan Fleiter. 'As sad as it is, he is preserved in our minds at what was probably his peak. He doesn't grow old in our minds, he doesn't fade away and he is always larger than life. That's the legacy he will leave behind.'

In the days and weeks that followed John's death, those who knew him remembered him in their own way. For some it was his background in the northern suburbs of Melbourne, for others it was the way he did business or his broader philanthropic efforts. John was a very different person to different people.

Ahmed Fahour notes, 'I think people loved him because he was genuine. He once said that he couldn't imagine a higher honour or greater privilege than to serve the people of the northern suburbs. I think in the months after [John's death] so many of us, including thousands who didn't even know John, put life in a different perspective. We cherished our families a little more, we thought about our health a little more, we stood still a bit more often and reflected on those things that are really important.'

John's legacy was particularly important to property developer Daniel Grollo, given their many similarities. Both were sons of immigrant families to Australia and both were from the northern suburbs. They were also a similar age and successful in their own fields.

'John's story will always be part of Melbourne's folklore because it is unique', says Daniel. 'He had to jump a lot of hurdles to get where he was. There was his religion—he was one of the first Muslim business leaders in Australia. There was his poor background, coming from Broadmeadows. There was his ethnicity, coming as a young immigrant from Turkey. There was his own education, or lack of it. He didn't make it through university. If you add all of those things up, what a remarkable story. The key thing that John had was an idea; it was a belief that one day everyone would have a mobile phone. He was right, of course, and he pursued that idea with passion.

'John's success was created by his own efforts and he brilliantly personifies the belief that people can make the most of their opportunity if they work hard enough. That's what defines this country, that we all have the freedom to create something.'

John's relationship with Shane Warne may have been born out of the establishment of the Shane Warne Foundation, but it actually evolved into a connection between two fathers with daughters of the same age attending the same school in Brighton. 'The thing that I remember the most about John was that he was a fair dinkum guy, and very intelligent', says Shane. 'He was loyal and he was friendly, but he was just a knockabout sort of guy. He was a very warm person, he also made people feel important. People gravitated towards him. John was just a great guy. We all miss him.

'These days both Simone [Shane's ex-wife] and I are always there for Patricia. We see her and her kids often through our children and we'd do anything for them. Sometimes straight after a tragic death there are lots of people around, but it's ongoing support that is really important. It's like my good friend Glenn McGrath, who lost his wife, Jane. I ring him a lot just to chat and see how he and his children are doing.'

Reflecting on John's contribution to his own and the wider community, Eddie McGuire comments, 'When John passed away we lost a truly wonderful person who was a giant at everything he did and a truly free spirit. The amazing thing was he'd only just started to make his mark on the wider community beyond what he did at Crazy John's, with his charitable work and his new allergy foundation. I think given enough time John would have touched every aspect of society.'

According to Ayse, the secret to John's success was in his genes, as well as his drive and energy. 'From Mum John inherited acute instincts about what was right and what was going to work. From Dad he inherited calmness, wisdom and the ability to display a philosophical side that everything was going to be okay. Dad also had the charisma to attract people that John had in spades.'

John's mother Nezaket fondly recalls a loving child. 'John was not a greedy or selfish man', she says. 'Money didn't drive him. John was a good person who cared about people.' His father Ali says the image of all the people at the funeral will stay with him forever. 'At the funeral—you judge people by how many people come and what impact you had on their lives', he says. 'I've been to funerals when I was the only one there. At John's funeral it was clear how many people had been affected by knowing John. The number of people who were there was a great comfort.'

The last word must go to John himself: 'I think we should all be judged by our actions—that's all'.

Chapter 3

1   M Charles, 'Crazy John from battler to tycoon', *The Daily Telegraph*, 23 October 2007.

2   In the 1980s, university political clubs were a hotbed of activisim.

3   *Catalyst*, television program, ABC Television, Sydney, 29 March 2007.

Chapter 5

1   Newswire, 'Mobile users top 3.3 billion', *The Sydney Morning Herald*, 25 May 2008.

Chapter 8

1   AAP, 'Two apartments at The Block in Bondi sold', 16 August 2003.

2   M Warner & E Whinnett, 'Crazy idea! The high-rise mobile phone king's $40 million dream', *Herald Sun*, 28 October 2005, p. 3.

Chapter 9

1 K Nicholas, 'Crazy John's steps into ring with Telstra', *Australian Financial Review*, 18 May 2004, p. 17.

2 G Barker, 'Crazy John's plans to abandon Telstra', *The Age*, 8 September 2005, p. 1.

Chapter 10

1 C Nader, 'A little girl's fate almost sealed with a kiss', *The Age*, 9 May 2006.

Chapter 11

1 M Warner, 'Just a suburban boy', *Herald Sun*, 3 May 2008, p. 90.

Chapter 12

1 J Thomson, 'Parting shots', *BRW*, 14 September 2006.

Chapter 14

1 J Thomson, 'Parting shots', *BRW*, 14 September 2006.

Printed in Australia
17 Nov 2017
653423